I0508070

THE ALCHEMIST OF NETWORK MARKETING

José Antonio Doménech
Ángels Muñoz

Copyright © 2017 José Antonio Doménech - Ángels Muñoz
Cover Design: Copyright © 2017 DomenikoArt

All rights reserved.

ISBN: 9798649295314

1º Edition: September 2017

2ª Edición: January 2019

English translated Edition: May 2020

Any reproduction of this book, in whole or in part, its incorporation into a computer system and its transmission in any form whatsoever by any medium, whether electronic, mechanical, photocopying, recording or any other method, is prohibited without the prior written consent of the publisher. Non-observance of the aforementioned rights may constitute a criminal offence of copyright infringement.

Disregard of the aforementioned rights may lead to legal action.

Content

Forewords…………………………………	5
The Accident……………………………	11
The mysterious Joseph Goodman………......	17
The Big Leap……………………………	31
Learning to Learn………………………..	45
The Lever………………………….......	61
Food for the Soul………………………..	83
An Unforgettable Basket...………………......	95
The Thinking Corner.....………………......	117
The Magic Fulcrum……………………..	129
The Immortals………………………....	145
Mega Clients…………………………….	157
The Stone and The Moon..………………....	173
The School and the Letter………………….	185
Addendum 1: The Levers…………………..	203
Addendum 2: The Traps……………………	205

Thanks,
Thanks,
and Thanks.

(You'll understand as you read it…)

Foreword by the Networker

In my more than ten years as a networker in one of the world's most successful network marketing companies, I have observed that people usually make the same mistakes over and over again.

I have also noticed how quickly they forget the advantages and benefits this business has to offer.

These circumstances have led me to ask Jose Antonio to write a brief text that clearly explains these basic concepts for new sales representatives. I never thought that we would end up with a book of the quality of this work.

Initially it was intended as internal material, but in view of the result we decided to make it available to all people who wanted to take advantage of its contents.

I was able to see with my own eyes how this book, with its moving history and the vivid examples in many who have read it, has brought about a whole new attitude and a changed view of business.

It is a reference book for people in leadership positions like myself, with large teams, as well as for newcomers to the business, and it is a good idea to read it over and over again.

It inspires and motivates us, and also provides us with

numerous examples of our presentations and meetings. I cannot thank Jose Antonio enough, whose first work this book is, for his intellectual effort. He has succeeded in eliciting this unforgettable story from the keys of his computer and his sharp mind, a story that is above all useful for our daily work in network marketing. Moreover, it is written in such an entertaining and appealing way that, as he puts it, "one will not only read it, but experience it".

Any tool that helps us find our inner peace and realise our dreams is worth activating.

I myself am a living example that if we follow the right guidelines WE CAN ACHIEVE EVERYTHING.

I hope you get the most out of the whole book so that your business finally gets going and you can achieve all your goals, both financial and personal.

Ángels Muñoz,
International Platinum Diamond
(4life Research)

Foreword by the Alchemist

First of all, I want to congratulate Angels for being the first 4Life distributor to recently achieve the highest rank of "International Platinum Diamond" in Europe. His tireless effort and innate vocation to help his distributors have made this important feat possible. My highest appreciation and admiration for it.

In this second edition of the book, I would like to begin by making something clear. The story is very similar to the first edition, but in addition to a new cover, this version brings another significant change. Whilst I was named as the sole author of the book in the first edition, you will notice that this time Angels Muñoz appears as co-author. Although she was against it, she is more than entitled to be named, as the book is based on her experience as a highly successful network marketing entrepreneur. Our two contributions to its creation were different, but essential to the final result you hold in your hands.

I have never met such a unique person in my life as her. No one else I have met has pursued the concept of assistance so consistently without expecting anything in return. This is one of the many virtues that has brought her so far in her network marketing company. The more than six thousand people from different countries that make up her team today can confirm my opinion.

I had the opportunity to witness at close range how she took up every just cause. In addition, I became a much better person in the years I was allowed to spend in close contact with her, for which I am deeply grateful.

This book is the result of all this "field experience", paired with my preference to explain complex relationships using simple examples.

Practicing "mental alchemy" is almost indispensable to progress in any area of life. To draw the hidden positive from any experience that seems to be an obstacle at first sight is a skill that we should all learn. I believe that this is the only way to achieve a happy life. The wise are experts in this ancient art. "Mental viruses", which you will read about in the following pages, confront your business as the main enemies and are thoroughly real, while the only antidote is mental alchemy.

If this book helps in any way to make you a little bit wiser and definitely get started in your business, my efforts to write it have more than paid off.

Now I don't want to steal any more time from you, so that you can get into the speedy beginning of the story. I hope you like it.

José Antonio Doménech

entrepreneur and writer

*"Abominable is the spiritual stinginess
of those who know and
do not pass on that knowledge"*

Miguel de Unamuno

*"There is nothing to fear in life,
you just have to understand everything.
Now is the time to understand more,
so that we fear less"*

Marie Curie

The Accident

– What a disaster! – I say to myself like an idiot again and again after I have accompanied Juan and his wife to the front door, said goodbye to them and thanked them for coming. Another presentation without closing! Why can't people see the opportunity I'm giving them?

– As Sara has already told me, these network marketing deals benefit a few at the expense of fools like me! – I continue my self-talk as I search for the car keys to make it to the supermarket before closing time.

All sorts of mopey thoughts come to my mind and take up almost all my attention. As if by magic, I get to the car, start the engine and head for the shopping centre.

After a few minutes of driving, the traffic seems to be calm, some drive out of town, others into town. The movement of the coloured cars has the same effect on me as the flow of blood through veins and arteries. Lost in thought, I notice a car overtaking me from the corner of my left eye. Everything seems to be going on properly, except for one small detail that shakes me out of my submersion in a matter of seconds.

– What is this? – I scream and honk like crazy.

The car is not about to overtake me, but is on the opposite lane of the expressway in the wrong direction. A ghost driver!

For a moment, I wonder if he really wants to kill himself or if it's just a very dangerous mistake. Unfortunately, both variants occur with great regularity.

I must warn him. So, I unlock the door on his side and hold a handkerchief out of the window while I continue to honk the horn. I can even see the young fellow in profile. He stares at the street as if he hasn't noticed anything.

– Is this guy stupid or deaf? – I scream in disgust.

Or is he actually suicidal? The mere possibility makes me shiver all over.

Still with goose bumps I see another vehicle approaching from a distance of about two hundred meters. It seems to overtake someone else right in the lane in which this stupid man is driving, on a direct route to ruin.

– No, no...! – I scream in a desperate attempt to make myself heard.

My heart is beating wildly, and out of desperation I keep turning the headlights on full beam so that the ghost driver slams on his brakes and moves to the side.

At the last moment, he obviously recognised the situation and tried to brake, but too late. Before I even know what is happening to me, I see the huge vehicle flying through the air over the central reservation and coming straight towards me! Clearly, it is my turn today. I will die.

This thought triggers a deep silence in me, which seems to last forever, until a loud bang pulls me out of my lethargy. Then I completely lose control of the steering wheel. I don't know how, but the pictures start to turn in countless glowing sparks. Again, the thought comes to my mind that I am going to die. In my mind's eye, all the things that I have been putting off for years are rushing by, believing that a better moment will come. I also recognise the faces of my wife and parents. And I, as a fool, have postponed all our projects together!

And, after many rollovers, with roaring noise and electrics sparking everything becomes quiet. A deep silence spreads. Since I feel no pain, I logically assume that I am dead. First I move one arm, then the other. But if this is death, it has a great deal in common with life. I am still perfectly buckled in my seat and the seat belt can be released without difficulty. So far, incredibly, everything seems to be okay. When I open the door, I notice that it opens much too easily. A little dazed and dizzy I get out and inspect the car. Well, what is left of it, because half of it is missing! There is no trace of the rear seats and the trunk, as if they had been cut off with a circular saw. In view of this surreal sight, I am totally baffled.

And how am I doing? Am I bleeding? Am I broken? I'm palpating my body, there's no blood anywhere. Arms and legs move, everything seems fine except for a pain in my neck. I can hardly believe it.

– I'm fine, thanks...! – I try to tell myself.

While I am still trying to grasp, what has happened, an alarming thought comes to me. The driver of the other car! In search of the vehicle I turn my head backwards jerkily.

– Ouch! – Immediately, a lashing pain runs through my neck. I have to be careful. Despite the pain, I run towards a bent and ruined piece of crash barrier where the vehicle must have hit. Before that, the torn-off half of my car gives me a shock when I pass it and it is now lying in the middle of the road. I think I'm going crazy, this can't be true! I try to push the thoughts with my car aside and continue my way to the crash barrier.

Once there, I see the car wedged into a big tree. Smoke is rising from various places. I look around for help, but as incredible as it may seem, there is no one to be seen for miles around. I rummage around in my trouser pocket to get out my mobile phone and call for help. But it is simply not there, I must have left it in the car. Should I get it? After a short thought, I see the first flames as I look at the car.

– My goodness, it is burning! – I stumble and look around again in the hope that someone will come to our aid. But in vain, there is nobody. I am on my own and have no time to lose. I must get these people out as soon as possible.

Without paying attention to the pain in my neck, which strangely enough is hardly noticeable anymore, I make my way through the bushes to the car. He is about thirty metres away, where I arrive with several scratches through the thorns of the bushes.

There is a smell of petrol in the air, which is not good. Now it is time to act. I quickly make my way to the driver's side, where I find an elderly gentleman alone in the car through the window. He is unconscious and blood is running down his face.

– Shit! – I am shocked when I notice a stronger flame emerging from the bonnet, which is completely wedged into the tree. Time is running out! The car could explode at any moment.

– Come on, hurry...! – I try to light myself up... It can't be that I got away unscathed so far and now I'm going to die! This can't be happening! – I continue my self-talk and search for the door handle... Oh my God, give me strength! – ... I pray as I find the right position to pull with all my might.

To my surprise, the door opens so easily on my violent jerk that the rebound makes me fall into a thorny bush. Due to the stress situation and my panic I hardly feel the scratches. I quickly straighten up again and go back to the door, which is now completely open. I push the airbag to the side as best I can and reach for the seatbelt buckle. It is stuck. Again, and again I push, but the belt does not release and the fire continues to spread. Again, thoughts of dying come to my mind.

Having almost surrendered to my fate, a discovery makes me optimistic again. I stretch out my right hand as far as I can for a pair of garden shears under the seat.

And indeed – in my hand is a beautiful pair of garden scissors, with a superb blade that makes it easy to cut the belt. After I have removed it, I grab the unconscious body on my right shoulder, turn around and stomp clumsily away through the bushes. No idea where I get the strength from, but somehow, I make it to the road. I climb up the embankment, where finally some people are running towards us. They help me to lay the injured gentleman on the ground with the greatest care. I too – overcome by dizziness – let myself fall.

– I'm a doctor! – there's a male voice.

The next moment I hear a loud explosion, followed by a hot blast. I see some people lying on the ground and siren sounds and coloured lights come through to me. Someone is talking to me, but I can't hear them well. I want to say something myself, but I can't get a word out. As if I were drunk, everything begins to spin around me. The face of the person opposite becomes blurred and everything dissolves. I immerse myself in a complete silence, and finally everything becomes dark.

Sounds come to my ear. That must be Sara, who prepares breakfast to get me going like every morning – Ouch! – a violent pain runs through my neck and flank.

– Sara! – I shout and try to remove something from my face.

– What the hell is that on my face and around my neck? – I'm whining. As I look around, I realise, stunned, that I am not lying in my bedroom.

– Where am I? Sara! – I'm starting to get nervous.

– It's all right, darling. – I finally hear the soft voice of my wife. Then she enters the mysterious room, accompanied by a man in a white coat. Hello, darling! Finally, you woke up! How are you feeling?

– Fine, I guess. My head hurts a little. But where are we?

– In the hospital, darling. You've had an accident. This is Dr. Marquez.

– You needn't worry, Mr. Guzmán – the doctor assures me in a deep voice. – Apart from a few harmless bruises, thank God you only have a pulled neck. You are very lucky because, from what I have been told, it is a true miracle. Your mild amnesia is normal after such an impact. It will pass quickly. What you need now is rest.

– The car! – I am surprised when a few images of what happened appear in my head. The burning car! – I scream, and while I instinctively want to stand up, a lashing pain drives through my neck.

– Calm down, please. Your body and mind need rest – the doctor tries to calm me down while he gently pushes me back into bed. Try not to move your neck violently. You must wear the neck brace for at least ten days. We know what you have risked to save the second driver involved in the accident. To put your mind at rest, I can tell you he's fine. You were both very lucky.

– Thank God, then at least it was worth it! – I am relieved.

– So, ladies and gentlemen, from tomorrow on, you can relax at home, because that's where it works best. However, to be on the safe side, I would prefer it if you stayed in the hospital tonight for observation.

– All right, doctor, thank you very much – answers Sara with a tender look at me.

As soon as the doctor is outside the door I immediately turn to her. – Sara, do you know anything more about the other driver?

– I have the same information as you, dear, and I want him to be all right, thanks to your courage. You're a real hero. Some of the eyewitnesses told me everything. I'm so proud of you, but you need to rest now.

The sofa for visitors does not look very inviting, so I persuade Sara to go home to sleep. I stay alone with the strange noises of the devices in the room. Little by little the images come together in my consciousness, at first wildly jumbled. Piece by piece, however, I manage to put the pieces of the puzzle together. When I remember the sight of the injured gentleman, everything contracts again within me. However, I cannot reconstruct his face.

The mysterious Joseph Goodman

After a week of rest at home I am already in much better shape. The headaches have almost disappeared, the bruises on the side had taken on all colours at first and are now slowly fading. And again, I spend more time without the ruff than with the thing around my neck. Several colleagues at work have inquired about my condition, but I don't feel like talking to anyone. Thanks to Sara as my bodyguard I only had to talk to my parents and my boss. Even a few colleagues from my network marketing company called my home to see how I was doing. It's amazing how news travels.

– Honey, what do you want to eat?

– Well, it doesn't matter. You know I don't have much of an appetite. Maybe some chicken and... The ringing of the phone interrupts my food selection.

– Honey, could you get that, please? Who do you think that is again?

Suddenly, Sara's head appears on the half-open bedroom door. She makes a strange grimace in my direction and holds her palm over the phone's microphone.

– What is it? – She made me curious... Who is it?

– It is Mr. Joseph Goodman.

– Who's that? I don't know him, he must have dialled the wrong number.

– No, he is the gentleman whom you helped in the accident – Sara enlightens me, comes over to me and stretches out the phone to me as a clear sign that I should accept the call.

Immediately my pulse rises and I notice a strange tension coming over me. I was not prepared for this moment, and now it has come without warning. For a moment, I am tempted to tell Sara to call back later, but then I instinctively reach for the phone.

– Hello...? Yes...? – it comes out of me a little hesitant.

– Hello... This is Joseph Goodman, the man you rescued from death nine days ago – a deep, warm voice welcomes me.

– Hello, Mr Goodman. How do you do?

– To tell you the truth, I have been through a healing process that is quite miraculous for my age. At least that's what the doctors say. But now I would like to know how you are.

– I am feeling much better. After you "landed" on my car I had a pulled neck and some bruises, but apart from that I am fine – I reply with a joking undertone.

– Ha-ha-ha! It's nice to hear you haven't lost your sense of humour. That's a good sign. You have no idea how happy this makes me.

– Yeah, I'm glad too, because that was really close.

– It was, and it's thanks to you that we got out in one piece. That's the second thing I wanted to talk to you about. I have been told what happened and I am infinitely grateful for the courage you have shown in this extremely difficult situation. You risked your life for an unknown, a sign of true human greatness.

– Well, anybody would have done that – I reply somewhat mechanically.

– Don't be so sure. However, that may be, fate intended us to share these moments together. That's why I would like to thank you and invite you and your wife to my house next Thursday for lunch. Of course, only if it suits you – he adds extraordinarily politely.

I don't really know how I should react. To be honest, I don't really feel like doing anything. But with so much kindness, I don't think I can resist.

– Of course, it's an honour for me – I'm not convinced.

– Very well, my wife and I will expect you on Thursday. Mary would like to meet you.

– The only problem is that my car is split in two – I admit jokingly ironic.

– Ha-ha-ha! I like your sense of humour. Don't worry, I'll have a chauffeur pick you up at noon sharp. Is that time OK with you?

– Yes, I think it suits me. It'll do me good to get out a little. Do you need our address?

– No need, I already got it at the hospital along with your phone number. We'll expect you for lunch on Thursday. All the best until then and thanks again!

– Until next Thursday, Mr Goodman – I still say goodbye in bewilderment.

Well, that wasn't so bad. Besides, I've been thinking about that man so much since the accident. Now he has a name, and on Thursday I hope to get to know him properly.

The following days pass quickly, and already the longed-for Thursday has arrived. I get up long before the alarm clock rings. I cannot sleep as excited as I am. Today I will meet Joseph Goodman.

I hope the chauffeur has no trouble finding our house. It is exactly 12:00 noon and we are almost ready. The moment I turn my eyes away from the kitchen clock, the doorbell rings. When I open it, a somewhat casually but impeccably dressed man with a broad smile on his face stands in front of me.

– Good afternoon, Mr. Guzmán, my name is Tom and I am to drive you to the Goodmans. As soon as you are ready, we can start – he greets me very relaxed.

– Yes, of course. Give us a minute, please.

– No problem, take as much time as you need. I'll wait for you in the car.

While I wait for Sara to fetch the mobile phone from upstairs, I take a look through the window out to the driver as he – if that's still possible – gives a gorgeous black four-wheel drive a high gloss finish.

– I'm ready, honey. Here we go! – tells me Sara when she reaches the bottom of the stairs.

At the car, the chauffeur awaits us smiling and holds the back door open for us. With a gesture, he invites us to get in.

Sara and I thank him in one voice.

– I have to thank you – the driver answers extraordinarily politely and closes the door.

We drive off without knowing the destination, which causes ambivalent feelings in me. On the one hand, I am a little worried because I am not in control of the situation. On the other hand, I feel transported back to a time long past, when the spirit of adventure was a trait of mine that has since been lost. I take Sara by the hand, we look at each other and smile.

– My feeling tells me that today will be a beautiful day – I whisper into her ear.

– I hope so – she answers slightly tense and with a doubting voice.

From the first part of the journey I conclude that we are heading south. We leave the city behind us and continue for about twenty-five minutes until we leave the main road and turn onto a rather bumpy secondary road. We have never been to this place before. The further we get, the further we seem to get into a valley of two mountains of the same shape that are getting closer and closer. In fact, the main road runs right between the two elevations, which now look like the pillars of gates to another world. Even the vegetation changes noticeably. I ask myself why we have never visited this area before. It is a thoroughly magical place, and I enjoy the expression on Sara's face, completely captured by the beauty of the landscape.

Finally, we reach a large wooden gate in a seemingly endlessly long wall, which makes me think of a huge country cottage. The rustic gate opens and allows us to enter a true paradise. No matter which direction we look, we are enchanted by the beauty and harmony of the plant and flower arrangements.

– We almost made it – Tom lets us know.

Sara and I look at each other like two children about to discover something completely new. I'm glad I came. Since the accident, we have been relatively settled, a little fresh air will have a tremendously positive effect.

In the distance, we recognise a wooden house. As we come closer we admire its size and the carved wooden elements. The house is beautiful. At the front door two people are waiting for us.

– Ladies and gentlemen, you can get out now! – Tom informs us after he has parked the car in front of the house. I am a little nervous, but Sara seems to have relaxed a bit.

– Shall we? – I ask Sara and nudge her when Tom opens the door for us.

– Welcome! – says a rich voice, which I recognise immediately. I know her from the telephone conversation, no doubt about it. – Thank you very much for coming!

I look up and face an older gentleman with completely greying hair, but athletic and elegant in appearance. At his side is a woman a few years younger, she too is very pretty and distinguished.

– You must be Mr Goodman – I notice and stretch out my arm to shake his hand.

– In person! Call me Joe, please. This is my wife, Mary – he replies, putting his arm around the waist of the woman next to him – And you must be Mr. Guzmán.

– Yeah, but for you, Jorge. May I introduce my wife Sara. – I say, and am amazed by his strong handshake. For his age I am guessing, he seems in impeccable shape.

– How was the trip? – Mary inquires courteously.

– It was fine. Very pleasant. Much better than the last time I got into a car. Besides, Tom prefers to keep the tyres on the asphalt.

– Ha-ha-ha! Your sense of humour is great, Jorge – answers Mr Goodman.

General laughter breaks out. My ironic joke has obviously managed to break the ice a bit.

– Please come in. A refreshment would come in handy in this heat. Would you care for a glass of fresh lemonade, which I have just made?

– Very much– one can hear Sara and me saying in unison again.

As I enter, I am surprised to find that the house is less luxurious than I had expected. But with the warm light it seems very cosy. The wonderful smell of food that characterises the ambience makes my mouth water. Everywhere in the room there are small details that probably all tell their own story. The walls are adorned with numerous pictures, but there is one in particular that attracts my attention: Mr. Goodman with Frank Sinatra, both of them in swimming trunks!

– Did you know Frank Sinatra personally? – I inquire slightly perplexed.

– Of course, I did! We were good friends – I'm amazed at how harmlessly he tells me that.

– Sara, can I steal Jorge for a moment while Mary shows you around the house? -. – I'd like to talk to him privately about something.

– Yes, of course, Sara. Just please bring him back to me.

We all laugh while Joe takes two filled lemonade glasses and asks me to accompany him outside. Obediently, I follow him. I wonder what could be so secret that we have to be alone for this.

– I want to walk a little and talk to you – he explains to me on the porch stairs down to the garden. – Walking stimulates the conversation, and I might as well show you around the property a bit.

His choice of words reminds me of a Mexican work colleague. The accent also sounds Mexican, although the name Goodman seems to come more from the USA. A friend of Sinatra's, so he must be American. I step outside and am completely absorbed in my pondering. I should probably ask him.

– Where are you from, Joe?

– Well, it's a long story. I'll tell you all about it one day, but in a nutshell, I was born in Mexico. My father was American and my mother Mexican, so I have both nationalities. Until the death of my parents, I commuted back and forth between the two countries.

– Oh, I'm sorry.

– Don't worry, that was a long time ago. It's about something else now. I invited you to my home because I am very grateful for the courage you showed that day and saved my life. And my intuition tells me there's a good reason why fate arranged for our paths to cross.

– Hmm, I don't know.

– What do you do in life, Jorge?

– I'm an accountant at a furniture manufacturing company.

– How's that working out for you?

– Well, the work's pretty boring and not very well paid. But that's the way it is. My wife thinks I should consider myself lucky to have a steady job.

– And aren't you trying to earn something in your spare time?

– Yes, well... – ... I reply with little conviction.

– But what? – he goes into it with a challenging voice.

– I don't know if you've heard of network marketing, a few months ago I got into a business where a few smart guys make money at the expense of dumb guys like me – I explain a little contrite. – And as I've been told, things are far from perfect.

– Eureka! – I hear him murmuring, while at the same time he puts on a big smile.

– Obviously, you are enjoying my failure – I accuse him slightly annoyed.

– Oh, no, no, no. I would never in my life take pleasure in something that was disadvantageous to you. I apologise if I gave you that impression. It's just that everything has become clear to me.

There's a pleasant female voice in the distance. – Please, come to the table. – Mary announces lunch is ready.

– Come along, dear. Mary's a great lady, but when the food gets cold, she's not to be trifled with. Ha-ha-ha! Let's go, or she'll be angry – he announces and takes a quicker step.

– Yes, all right, but what is the "all" you just understood?

– Not right now, soon you'll understand. For now, relax and enjoy your meal. Mary's a first-class cook.

A little disturbed at the prospect of an unanswered question, I follow him into the house, where the smell is even more seductive than before. My appetite and the stimulating conversation with the ladies push the events into the background.

After a fantastic feast and interesting conversations, Joe and I go to the veranda again while Mary and Sara prepare tea.

– Do you believe in the "causality" of fate? – Joe wants to know from me.

– Did you mean "casualty" or "causality", Joe?

– Ha-ha-ha! Although the two words are quite similar, their meanings are opposite, coincidence versus causality. Perhaps you can imagine more under the notion "synchronicity", as Jung called it, or simply "signs".

At the moment, excerpts from the book "The Alchemist" by Paulo Coelho, which I had read years ago, come to my mind.

– Do you refer to "signs" as in Coelho's book "The Alchemist"?

– That's right, it's a wonderful book. Have you read it?

– Yes, a long time ago. But I didn't pay much attention to that aspect of it.

– Well, let me tell you something. In our new relationship, everything is undoubtedly a sign, or as I like to call it, a causality. You wait years for this, and to be honest with you, I thought you'd never show up.

– I'm sorry, I'm not sure I understand you, Joe.

– Don't worry, you'll understand bit by bit. Earlier, you said something to which I responded with "eureka".

– Yes, and it's been disturbing to me, too.

– I apologise, but there's a time for everything. Life is capricious. Suddenly the scales fell from my eyes when you told me you were trying out network marketing.

– And what does that have to do with us?

– Come with me, Jorge, I want to show you something.

We enter the house again where Joe asks me to take two cups from the table and follow him. We use the stairs to climb up to the first floor, from where we continue to the second floor. There

I find an incredible room. As you can easily tell from the central table and the arrangement of chairs and armchairs, we are in his office. The walls are decorated with all kinds of photos and prizes, as well as various awards and honours. A large oblong window serves as a source of light, allowing a view of the surrounding paradisiacal landscape. The harmonious structure is completed by a light, delicate curtain, which weakens the light rays arriving from the side without restricting the beautiful view.

– Please take a seat – he points to a seating area with upholstered armchairs opposite the table. – I see you are a good observer. Therefore, you most certainly have not failed to notice that I had no problem with money and success.

– Apparently not.

– It wasn't always that way. He pauses and looks up at the ceiling. I want to tell you something. When my parents died, I was placed in an orphanage and later in other institutions because we had no close relatives. This went on until I was of age. When I left this world, I got into trouble wherever I could. Everything went wrong and I was a magnet for all kinds of problems. I experimented with drugs, almost fell into alcohol and even lived on the streets for a while. I was a disaster as a human being. But one day, about your age, a very strange thing happened to me.

– A causality! – I interject.

– You might say that, or at least one of many. Listen carefully, you'll soon understand.

– That day I woke up on a park bench. With the hangover from the booze the night before and the realisation that the last bit of money had been stolen from my pocket, I fell into an absolute depression. I was pessimistic, my life no longer had any meaning. So, I made the "brilliant" decision to put an end to it.

– You wanted to commit suicide? – I ask in astonishment at his cheerfulness.

– Yes, exactly, I wanted to kill myself and was completely convinced of my decision. There was no reason to continue to fight, life had turned against me. I felt at the end of my strength. So, I went to a cliff where I usually admired the beauty of the ocean to put an end to all my troubles. The almost one hundred metres down should be dead certain, I thought. I stood on the edge and said a farewell prayer. But a small part deep inside me wanted to live on. So, before I finally plunged down I asked infinity to give me a clear sign, if it was not yet time to die.

I can't believe that this so self-confident man should have gone through such an extreme and desperate situation. I would like to ask him what he means by infinity, but I hold myself back. I don't want to interrupt him. After a short pause for a talk and a sip of tea he continues.

– Nothing happened for about five minutes, after which I came to terms with the fact that the time had come. And just at the moment I closed my eyes and wanted to jump off, a huge bang sounded, followed by numerous others. When I turned around, a car rolled over several times in the air and spun towards me. I stood there frozen, thinking for a moment that the suicide was over because I was being crushed by this approaching mass. But miraculously the car made one last turn and hit the ground three or four metres in front of me. I was rooted to the ground and my muscles would not obey me until I heard something that sounded like cries for help. Then life came into my body again and I rushed to the voice's aid. The vehicle had come to a halt at the side, so the driver's door pointed upwards, where the roof should actually be. While I tried to get there, the car went up in flames.

– Oh, dear! In our case you were unconscious, yet this story is more and more similar to what we experienced – it escapes me as I eagerly await the sequel. – And then what happened?

– Well, the fire and the acrid smell of petrol didn't look good. I had to get this gentleman out as quickly as possible or we would both die. To my own amazement, I made a point of preserving my life, which I had wanted to throw down the cliff a few minutes earlier. To be honest, I do not remember how I did it and where I got the strength from, but I managed to free this man from the car and get him away from where a huge ball of fire rose shortly after.

He stands up and hands me a framed photo showing him in a visibly younger age with an older man. They hold each other in a familiar and friendly manner around their shoulders.

– Yes, that is me in earlier years. Don't look at me like that, I know myself that time is relentless – he says smiling. – But please pay attention to the gentleman next to me. He is Don José, the driver of the car from that time.

— So, you saved his life in the end? — I ask about it with interest.

— Yeah, and not only that. He became the most important person in my life, my best friend and, more importantly, my mentor.

— Your mentor? Your mentor for what?

— You know, Jorge, this gentleman was known in the USA as "The Great Networker", because of his resounding success in the network marketing industry, which I didn't know at all at that time.

— Network marketing? Are you talking about multi-level marketing? — I ask and put one and one together at the same time.

— Yes, I am talking about multi-level business. Do you see all the awards and recognitions on the walls? Many of them are from my multi-level business, as you call it. I earned them by following the steps and guidelines given to me by Don José. As he proved to me, success comes from understanding things and, above all, approaching them in a certain way.

— Hmm... Multi-level... the sign... your mentor — I mumble to myself and try to put the pieces of the puzzle together.

— That's right. I offer to teach you the key elements that first Don José taught me and later the years of experience.

— I don't know what to say — I shudder. Joe has completely thrown me off my game.

— You don't have to rush into anything. Think about it calmly. I don't need an answer now. But I would like to point out one thing, as Don José did with me when he offered himself as my mentor — he explains with a glance at the photo. — He said to me: "When you get involved, you must be prepared to look at sides of yourself that you did not want to know in the first place. I will confront you with things that you do not want to hear. And I will ask you to do things you don't want to do at all. If you accept my offer, you have to be willing to pay the price. And I'm not talking about money.

— Thank God, because I'm broke anyway.

– How do you think my bank balance was when I met Don José? Worse than yours now, I can assure you.

– If you're not talking about money, what price are you talking about?

– There will be plenty of opportunities to explain, but just as a foretaste, I would like to tell you that in order to excel in something, you must give up some things that feel comfortable. In return, you must begin to tackle others that you do not feel comfortable with. Not everyone is ready for this.

I don't know what to say and I ponder. The truth is that the price Joe is referring to is actually high, but in my opinion it is no worse than the feeling of defeat I carry around with me. I may be able to get the help I have so often longed for. I must seize this opportunity.

– I accept! – is my impulsive response.

– Not so fast, my friend! Before you inform me of your final decision, there are a few things I'd like to discuss with you. If you still want to be a part of it, you'll have to sign a document. Could you come alone tomorrow?

– Sure, but...

– Perfect!

– But, Joe, I don't quite understand about signing a document. What's all this about?

– You'll find out tomorrow. Just be patient. I've had enough for today. We'd better get down to the women before they get mad at us. Ha-ha-ha!

We go downstairs and kiss our wives as if on cue. The rest of the afternoon we talk about this and that, but the conversation never comes back to the topic of network marketing. Mary and Joe are two entertainers, educated and with highly interesting views. Mary and Sara have also found a very good connection to each other, and I'm glad to see that my wife feels comfortable. For my part, I cannot get away from my conversation with Joe in his office.

Afterwards we all step out onto the veranda to say goodbye to each other. We thank them exuberantly for their hospitality and issue a return invitation to our home whenever they want.

– We both have work to do tomorrow. Is it all right with you if Tom comes to pick you up at ten? – Joe reminds me of our date when we shook hands.

Sara, who knows nothing about our conversation, looks at us astonished and at the same time angry because I made plans without telling her.

– I'll explain it to you later, darling – I say to her in a conciliatory tone, which, however, does nothing.

– Please do not be angry, Sara. Allow me to take Jorge away from you for a few hours. We have a few things to talk about, but he'll be back by noon, I promise – Joe tries to calm Sara down, whereupon her expression relaxes a bit.

– Thanks again for the wonderful food, we really enjoyed it very much.

– Thank you very much! See you tomorrow. Oh, I almost forgot: Come in comfortable clothes – Joe instructs me.

– I'll see you tomorrow. Are we going on a trip?

– Ha-ha-ha! Something like that, Jorge – he replies with a mischievous look.

After a last wave through the car window, we leave the property behind and drive back home, while I go through the conversation with Joe again and again in my mind.

The Big Leap

The doorbell rings at ten o'clock sharp. How does Tom manage to get here on time? I quickly take my last sip of coffee.

– Darling, I'm off – saying goodbye to Sara.

– Bye, and be careful not to hurt yourself on the trip – considering my sporty clothes she gives me some motherly advice.

– Don't worry, darling. I'll take care of myself – I respond on my way out. Good afternoon, Tom, may I offer you a cup of coffee?

– Hello, Jorge. No, thank you. Very kind of you. If you don't mind, I'll wait for you in the car.

– No need, I'm all ready. Let's go, Tom!

Once again, I get into the immaculate four-wheel drive from the day before, but this time I take a seat in the passenger seat next to Tom. We start off in the same direction as yesterday, so I suppose we're going back to the country house. The driving time passes in no time due to the conversation with Tom and my thoughts, which mainly revolve around this meeting with Joe.

– Good morning, Jorge! – I hear Joe's characteristic voice as I get out of the car.

– Hello, Joe.

– Come on in, Jorge. – ... he calls out to me and grabs me by the shoulder. – Let's step into my office for a moment. We have something important to do.

At the top of the stairs we sit down opposite each other at the magnificent wooden desk. On the side, closer to me I notice a document. Since I do not want to appear curious, I pretend not to have noticed it.

– I told you about what you were looking at yesterday.

– You mean the contract? – I'm playing dumb.

– I wouldn't call it a contract, more like an "agreement".

– An agreement between you and me?

– Not exactly. – No? What else?

– Read it and you'll understand.

I pull the document towards me. Judging from the thickness and colour, it's not ordinary office paper. After putting on my glasses, I begin to read...

I AGREE WITH MYSELF:

1.- To keep my word when I give it.

2.- To be grateful for everything I have (and that is a lot), and also for the things I do not have.

3.- To be mercilessly honest with myself.

4.- To have full confidence in my abilities and those of others.

5.- To choose my words carefully and wisely.

6.- To do everything in my power for a great life

7.- To always be patient with myself and others.

8.- To forgive myself and others.

9.- To give my best at all times and in every task.

10.- Not to ask Joe for money or anything else, but to accept all gifts he deems necessary.

I, Jorge Guzmán, sign and give my word. (Remember point one of the agreement).

After reading through it several times, I have no words. I look Joe in the eye and I struggle through to a question:

– So, you want me to make a deal with myself?

– Rather, I would describe it as an agreement between your current self and the better version of yourself that you can become. Or rather, the one you are in the process of becoming, incredible as that may sound. Just trust me.

– The better version of myself I can become? – I can't hide my amazement.

– Yeah, you heard me, ha, ha, ha, ha... – he bursts out laughing again, the mocking tone does not sit well with me. You know, Jorge, in one way or another we are all artists, and our lives represent our masterpiece. Its quality depends on ourselves. We are all sculpture and sculptor at the same time.

As I think about it, my old fears are starting to surface. So many negative things have already happened to me, so I do not want to be manipulated or deceived again.

– I don't know. When I enter into an agreement, I want to keep it, but there are some points where I am not sure I can do so.

– Are you satisfied with your work of art, that is, your life? – he follows up. – Do you think you've done your best? Or better yet, are you doing your best right now?

– No, of course not – I'm responding a little grumpy. – Sure, I have much more to give, but...

– But, but, but... – Joe interrupts me abruptly. – That means you don't want to make a deal with yourself and your life, right? If I'm wrong, you can safely sign the document and we'll be able to move on.

– It's just that I'm worried I won't be able to keep all the terms of the agreement.

– So, it scares you to make a deal with yourself. The poor, misunderstood fear has such a bad reputation, but we will come to that later. But now come, I take you to a place you'll like.

– For which I should come in comfortable clothes?

– That's right, ha, ha, ha ...

– So, I don't have to sign anything?

– What do you think? – He answers halfway out the door as if I hadn't said anything. – Come on, come on! Tom is waiting for us at the car.

We go downstairs and get in the 4x4 in front of the house. This time we're going in another direction, the property is just huge. Every new place we pass seems more spectacular. I even discover a small lake where a man is fishing.

– The place is incredible, Joe, and the lake is really beautiful.

– Yeah, you're right. It's what Mary and I dreamed of. Exactly as you see it in front of your eyes, the little paradise of our dreams has come true. I'll show it to you in more detail, but let me go back to the conversation we had earlier. How often has it happened that something has scared you off and you have withdrawn in the face of a situation or challenge that frightens you?

– Certainly, more often than I would like – I notice with a bit of self-pity.

– Don't let yourself down, that's how most people feel. The problem is that fear is confused with "being scared off" even though they are two very different things. Feeling fear now and then is a good sign. It shows that you are becoming my friend. But if you let yourself be scared and run away, you will miss the reward.

– And what's the reward?

– In a great, fulfilled, courageous, that is, lived and not survived life – he becomes briefly thoughtful. – Don't you think an eagle chick is afraid of free fall on its first attempt at flight?

– I suppose so.

– Although he is an eagle, he is afraid of the unknown, just as you are – reluctant as Joe is to judge my life when he hardly knows me, but in this case, he hits the mark. – Do you like flying?

– Yeah, it's all right. – I lie, as I've always had problems with flying because of my fear of heights. I'm not supposed to look out the window because of my fear of heights – I add this in an attempt to be a little more honest.

– Fear of heights? Perfect.

– You think that's perfect? What's perfect about it? – once again, it becomes mysterious.

– Nothing, it has something to do with me – he evades my question and continues shortly thereafter. – You know, people carry all kinds of fears around with them and don't even know it. It's the same with you. My experience has taught me that there are two kinds of fears: The first type is necessary and natural, because it warns us of a dangerous situation. This fear is wonderful because it can save our lives. However, most fears are of the other kind, namely unfounded and inherited. They have been transmitted to us like a virus. And, what is worst of all, they are mostly passed on to us by the people we love the most, our family and our teachers. And then, of course, by society and television. Like everyone else, you believed what you were told. But the others were infected for a long time.

– A virus from my family? I had a good upbringing at home and they did everything they could so that I could study at university. Thanks to them I have a degree in economics – I protest strongly in an effort to stand up to him.

– This honours them and is fantastic. However, what I am talking about is not titles, but trust. Did they believe in you? Did they support you unconditionally in your personal plans, even if they did not agree to them? – he says and looks me firmly in the eye.

– I don't like to admit it, but in truth they never really believed in me. To be honest, I always missed that with my parents and also with my friends.

– Without realising it, they have, despite their good intentions, stunted your potential and therefore your dreams, by overwhelming you with prejudices and fears.

– They did as well as they could.

– I'm aware of that. The lack of trust in you by your family and friends comes from their own fears, which they have inherited from their family and society. I don't know if you are aware of this. As you have said, they did the best they could, but unfortunately, they believed their ancestors and you did the same with them later. Most of your unfounded fears are part of this process, which is repeated from generation to generation, similar to mental viruses. The problem with them is that they severely restrict us, they can turn us into cowards and conformists. Through them we get a very limited picture of ourselves and gain too little self-confidence. I ask you again: How often have you given up a project because of fear? Or rather, because you let yourself be put off by some fear?

There is silence in the car. The truth is, he's so right. The memories of all the projects that I didn't finish for countless reasons are buzzing around in my head.

– More than I care to say, Joe – I'm starting to feel uncomfortable. Instead of helping me, Joe seems to want to finish me.

– I don't want you to feel bad. It hurts to face the truth, I know that. But we don't have much time and we have to get right to the point. You know, one of those viruses is doing a lot of damage to our business. I'm talking about the fear of what you don't understand. That's why, during these days that we're going to spend together, I'm going to do everything I can to give you clarity on several crucial issues. The most important thing is that you understand.

– Understand what?

– Yourself, for example. Ha-ha-ha

– I'm getting a little tired of his laughter. Why are you working as an accountant? Because this job excites you, right?

– It doesn't inspire me at all, it bores me to death. And the worst thing is the pressure my boss puts on me all day long. But what can I do? At least it's a safe job – Joe is about to drive me crazy.

– Safe? Ha-ha-ha! Nothing in life is safe, son, unlike the stories they sold you to keep you permanently numb. It pays take the risk to live. People who are always looking for the safety you mentioned end up as zombies. A fixed income often leaves the mind stunted, my friend. Surviving life right or wrong has nothing to do with real life. The only chance we have to live is to seize it.

– Of course, but as my mother says: "Better devil you know than the uncertain good" – I counter to enforce my opinion.

– Ha-ha-ha! This saying is about the worst and most widespread of all fears, namely the fear of the unknown.

Remember what I told you, even the vernacular instils fear. This wisdom contains the recommendation not to risk anything. But I tell you that not taking risks is the greatest risk in life. The real question is obvious: Will you allow these fears to deter you all your life or are you tired of running away from yourself?

– Sure, but how can we put away what we have learned? There's gotta be a way, right?

– Yes, there is, and with courage, lots of courage. So, the question is, are you brave enough to fight it?

– Of course, I am. – I am very confident of my abilities.

– Perfect, because in just a few minutes you'll have the opportunity to prove it – he replies as we come to an area that looks more and more like an airfield to me.

– Are we gonna fly now? – I'm beginning to understand why he asked me if I like to fly.

– Yes, I want to show you something from above – he answers when leaving the car.

– Show me something from above? – my legs get all shaky. The few times I've boarded a plane, I couldn't even look out the window because of my fear of heights.

– I know, but... what about my fear? – I sound like a scared kid.

– Are you gonna let that scare you again? The fear of heights is nothing more than one of your fears, much like the fear that tied your hands so you wouldn't sign the agreement. We must begin to confront those fears that frighten you so much. Come on, otherwise we'll be on the ground!

Meanwhile, it is not only my legs that are shaking, my whole body is shaking. All I want now is to run away from here, but I can't. However, I do it, I have to get on that plane. As long as I don't look down, there is no problem, I have already done that on other occasions. Before the imminent take-off, I try to calm down. On wobbly legs, I climb into the plane and we are already in the air!

The pilot seems to know his business, because the take-off is very smooth. I let myself fall into a seat behind the pilot and concentrate on not looking out of the windows. Everything is fine with me, the floor, the ceiling or my seat. Anything but not looking out the window.

– Jorge, come to the back – Joe asks me a few minutes after take-off.

I loosen my seatbelt and go into the back of the plane, as Joe asked. There are some other people sitting next to him whom I hadn't even noticed because of all the flutter. We greet each other, but I am already dizzy, so I am not able to be too intense.

– Take a seat next to me, Jorge – I sit down next to Joe, who starts to adjust my clothing. Apparently, he's putting on something like a life jacket.

– What are you doing, Joe? What's this?

– Don't worry, it's just for jumping.

– It's only for jumping. Apparently, all the dizziness and noise made me not quite hear you.

– What did you hear?

– That this is just for jumping! No, it's the dizziness.

– You heard me. We're going to do a tandem jump. Don't worry, I've done it more than a thousand times.

What, I shouldn't worry? A thousand jumps? No, no way! That's out of the question. Flying is one thing, but jumping out of a plane is something else entirely. No, no, no...! – I'm not even dizzy from shock. This can't be happening.

– Where did your courage go, Jorge?

– This is just too much of a thing, you want me to die of a heart attack!

– You can believe me, if you conquer this fear, it will be much easier for you to deal with the rest. I admit this is a bit extreme, but as I told you before, I can't give you too much time. So, we'll have to skip some lessons. Prove your courage to yourself, then you will no longer be afraid to sign the treaty and we will get ahead in your training. I remind you again that we do not have much time.

– But what's the hurry? Why is there no time?

– In a short while I have a long journey to make, and I want you to get on with your life and business as quickly as possible. We can't wait, think of it as shock therapy.

– I can't do it, I'm not gonna jump...! – I scream as I notice the door opening and I catch a glimpse of the endless horizon before I close my eyes. I don't even want to look, unbelievable that I have to go through something like that.

– Do you remember the frightened eagle chick before its first attempt at flight that I told you about? – despite his strong voice, I find it hard to hear his words with so much wind and noise.

– Yes...! – I scream with my eyes closed while Joe puts on something that feels like glasses.

– Do you know what Eagle Mama does when she sees her chick's fear?

– No...! – I scream in panic.

– She pushes it out...! – calls Joe, just before I feel a push in my back, which catapults us both out of the plane despite my attempt to avoid it.

Then, after jerking the belt several times at different points, a strange feeling sets in. Deep silence spreads within me, at the same time I feel almost weightless. My mouth opens by itself and I find it difficult to breathe.

– Close your mouth a little – Joe's voice comes to my ear. – And above all open your eyes, now open them already! Ha-ha-ha! Be brave. Remember your courage. You can do it. Trust me. Have faith in me, my friend! – he calls to me with a strange sound in his voice.

I try to open my eyes behind the aerodynamic goggles that Joe has put on me without really noticing. Carefully I open them a crack and recognise small coloured squares. They must be fields.

Finally, I open them completely and after a huge initial fright I realise that the expected and dreaded fear of heights does not come true. On the contrary, when I look at the landscape I get into an almost meditative state. To my amazement, the feeling of weightlessness together with the view of the endless expanse of the horizon is transformed into something very pleasant. It is simply incredible. But suddenly the question arises in my head where my fear of heights has gone.

We remain in an almost mystical silence until the parachute opens after a sudden jolt and the speed drops significantly. Now it feels like hanging from the sky like a marionette.

– How was the free fall for you? – Joe wants to know about me.

– Awesome! It was the most incredible feeling in my whole life.

– I'm proud of you, and you should be. You have mobilised courage that you didn't even know you had. We'll talk more when the ground is back under our feet. Now let's just enjoy the view in peace.

Even with the parachute open, the flight is a pleasure, different and calmer, but no less delightful. I see the ground coming towards us faster and faster and I also recognise Tom next to the four-wheeler, stretching out his arms as if to greet us. I could never have imagined not suffering from fear of heights in such a situation. Now Joe makes sure with a masterly landing manoeuvre that everything is a piece of cake. After a small impact at the end I emit a loud scream, which probably expressed something like euphoria. I don't think I've felt like this since I was a child.

– Where's your fear of heights gone now, Jorge? – Joe's giving me that accomplished look.

– My vertigo? I don't know. I must have left it on the plane. Ha-ha-ha.

Joe swoops in, and finally we can laugh together. – Thank you, Joe – my eyes are moist with emotion as I turn to him – It was one of the most wonderful experiences of my life.

– You're welcome, but we still have some work to do. Let's take advantage of this pleasant and intense atmosphere you are in right now, so that you can finally make an agreement with yourself and your life.

– The agreement?

– Exactly! This moving moment is especially suited for this, because this way you will never forget it. Or are you still afraid to sign? – he smiles mischievously.

– No, I don't fear anything at this point, I think – full of verve and self-confidence I stand up. – Did you bring the document?

He stretches out his hand, and Tom hands him a folder, which he opens and takes out the sheet. Joe then pulls out an expensive fountain pen and hands it over to me with the folder. Without thinking about it, I enthusiastically put my signature under the text. When I want to return the fountain pen to him, Joe fights back with his hands.

– No, the fountain pen should be yours, as a reminder of this very significant moment in your life. I want you to guard it like the apple of your eye. It will be a great help to you in difficult moments, when some fear comes over you and wants to chase you away.

– But I can't accept it, it must have cost a fortune.

– What, you're in violation of the tenth rule of the agreement so soon? Ha-ha-ha...! – we all laugh while I hug Joe.

– Thanks again, Joe. It was a lesson I'll never forget.

– Thank you for your confidence in me. I realise how difficult this was. You faced your fear. It took a little help, like with the eagle. That's normal, and soon you'll be able to face your fears without help of any kind. You will even enjoy it, you'll see. Because of our fears, we miss wonderful things every day, from skydiving to declarations of love to family members. We humans are full of unfounded and learned fears. Because of this garbage, we miss out on much of life. Unfounded fears are the greatest enemy, they make the soul rust. They turn you into a zombie fighting for your very survival. The good news is that you can defeat them if you understand what they are and why they exist. Just never be put off when they appear, remember that. Come on, let's go. I gotta get you home for dinner. That's what I promised Sara, and a promise must be kept.

We're going back to the car.

– So, I've signed it now, which means we're good to go, right?

– We can proceed, if it is called so correctly. We started the night I landed on you and you saved my life.

– All right, let's get on with it.

– Do you want to know your first task? – he asks me after he's stowed the parachute in the boot and we've driven off.

– Sure.

– Your first task is also one of the most complicated. As we have a lot of topics to cover, I would like you to come early tomorrow, Saturday and stay with me until Sunday evening.

– Yes, but... You know, on Sundays I usually have dinner at Sara's parents' house. She won't be happy at all, because she holds these fixed points sacred.

– That's why I thought it was one of the most complicated tasks, ha, ha, ha! I tell you something, my dear. Life is about setting priorities. The way you prioritise is the way your life looks. Usually, for important things, you have to give up less important things. It's the law of life. Talk to Sara, and if she gets mad, it's no big deal. She'll understand soon, trust me.

– All right, she'll kill me, but let's see how I tell her.

– Tom will be at your place at 9:00 sharp, OK?

– Yeah, that figures. At nine sharp I'll be expecting him – without taking my eyes off the road, Tom raises his thumb as a sign of approval.

While I'm still thinking about what to tell Sara, we've already arrived home. As I say goodbye to Joe, I pull out the beautiful fountain pen and thank him again.

– Memorise two of the points of your agreement tonight. Oh, and please bring a notepad and pen. I want you to write everything down. Don José used to say, "A short pencil is better than a long memory".

– All right, Joe, I'll see you tomorrow.

– See you tomorrow, and I congratulate you again on your courage, Jorge – Joe says goodbye with a wink and slams the door of the four-wheeler, which is moving away quickly.

I'm still dazed by everything that happened today. Looking at the folder, I read the headline on the cover in capital letters that I had overlooked so far. Typical Joe:

"Arrangements with myself for a Great Life"

Learning to Learn

The next morning and after a proper argument with Sara I hear the doorbell again. Nine o'clock sharp, I realise with a glance at the clock. I open, and there stands the obviously always good-humoured Tom again with a smile in front of me.

– Good morning, Mr Guzmán! I hope you had a restful night!

– Good morning, Tom, yes, thank you very much.

– Take your time getting ready, I wait by the car.

I'm going to the kitchen to say goodbye to Sara. When I try to kiss her on the cheek, she turns away. She's mad because I didn't include her in my weekend plans. A little depressed because of the bad mood I leave the house.

– Are you all right, Mr. Guzmán? – Tom asks as he drives off.

– Yes, Tom, thank you. I'm just tired – I don't feel like giving him explanations about my relationship problems.

With Tom, the journeys pass in a pleasant way. He is an uncomplicated person who radiates peace and cheerfulness. In combination with the entertaining conversation this makes him the ideal travel companion. He also almost made me forget the conflict with Sara. When we arrive at our destination, I see Joe sitting on the veranda.

– Good day, Jorge! Come sit with me – he points to a chair opposite him.

– Good morning, Joe – after shaking hands with each other I sit down and discover a chessboard on the table, its pieces set up ready for a game.

– Do you play chess, Jorge?

– Yes, but I haven't done so for ages – my answer is not quite honest, because although I know how to move the different pieces, I can't really play.

– Perfect, then the game can begin!

– Let the game begin! – I answer and prepare to start the game. Maybe Joe is not a great chess master. I cling to this hope to cheer myself up.

The white pieces are on my side, so I move a pawn almost at random and try to give myself the appearance of being sure of myself. On the fifth or sixth move he draws his queen and surprises me with an announcement.

– Checkmate!

– Checkmate? Already? I don't believe it! – On closer inspection, I find that my king has no means of escape. All of my options are blocked by one of his pieces. Given my poor game performance, I look a little foolish.

– Listen, Jorge, success in life and business follows its own rules and strategies, just like in chess. The first thing Don José taught me is that success is an exact science. Some people think they know the rules, which may be partly true, but they don't put them into practice. But it is practice that makes perfect, and like you in this game, they do not get very far. Both life and success are part of a big game, where, like in chess, it is important to understand the rules. The emphasis is on "understanding", not just "knowing". I have already explained the crucial difference between knowing and understanding. If someone memorises something, he will forget it by the time, but if he really understands and internalises it, it will remain present forever. Therefore, in our days together I would like to try to make you understand the rules that will inevitably lead you to success in network marketing and in life. If you understand and internalise them from the bottom up, the practical implementation will inevitably follow.

– Good judgement is needed, my dear – he continues after he has had a sip of water. – All our subjects are exclusively about good judgement. Now we're really going to get started, so please take notes. Over the years, I've come to realise that network marketing business consists of two basic steps.

– From just two steps?

– Yeah, you want to know step one?

– Yes, please! – I ask him and get my writing materials ready.

– I call step one, "Learning to Learn. "

– "Learning to learn"?

– That's right. Step One is about learning things from a new perspective. You must learn to learn how your brain behaves, or it will continue to sabotage your plans. Of course, you also have to learn to control your emotions again, just like the fears we talked about yesterday. And you also have to relearn how to relate to others. That means you have to learn to learn in many areas. I warn you, all of this will not be easy and will require great effort on your part. However, if you understand certain concepts, everything will be much easier for you. It will be worth the effort, because the price you pay is far more than a good business. The real reward will be your life and yourself. Success in network marketing will come as a result of your new life.

– It would never have occurred to me to have to learn so many new things in this phase of my life – my voice cannot hide a certain irony.

– That's the problem, after all, that we humans think we already know everything. Incredibly, we often miss the most important things. Very often, when we look at things from a new angle, they are the most obvious ones. Let me give you an example: What do you think is the best product of your network marketing business?

– Well, our health products are excellent.

– Sure, no doubt. But they're not your best product.

– Ah, I see your point. Our best product is a compensation plan and the ability to create a passive income.

– That's certainly more important than the previous one, but that's not what I was talking about either.

– No? - After a moment's consideration. – Then, what do you think, Joe?

– Remember and never forget what I'm about to tell you: The most important product until you yourself!

– Me? Okay, but...

– And please understand first of all – he goes on – that life is like a mirror, a big magic mirror. Many people think that the secret to success lies in what they do. Of course, what they do also counts, but the results achieved and the actions taken only reflect who they are at heart, the person they have become. That means it is about their attitude towards life.

– Who they are at heart? It is decisive what we do.

– Of course, but for Step One to be successful, you need to do a number of tasks in a certain way and in a certain order, as we will discuss later. This is what is visible from the outside. However, if you don't understand how your brain and heart work, you won't understand anything and therefore won't be able to accomplish anything. The change has to start from your inner being. Nowadays, quantum physicists believe that everything is a matter of perspective, and they are right. Our perception of the world changes our reality and therefore our results in everything we do. This claim has been made by many in the context of spiritual growth, and scientists are now sharing this view. As I said before, it is an exact science.

– All well and good, but what good is it if the people I contact don't show up for business presentations or tell me it's all a scam?

– They just miss out. We'll talk about that in detail later. For now, I want you to understand that success in this business depends entirely on you. It is vital that you keep that in mind, my friend. The first step is always to look inward, that's the most important thing to understand. Forget what you may or may not think you know. Come with me, I want to show you something – we get up and I accompany him behind the house, where he points to two huge and beautiful potted plants.

– You see those plants?

– Yeah, sure, they're gorgeous.

– They didn't always do so well. When the florist brought the pots, they were already filled with earth. Later, Mary planted pretty specimens, but despite the best care, they unfortunately died. So, we removed them and put in new ones, which also did not survive. We couldn't explain it and planted a different kind of plant for the third time. Can you imagine what happened?

– I suppose they didn't survive it either? – I answer timidly, afraid to be wrong.

– Exactly! Then Mary came up with an idea as ingenious as it was simple, and it solved the problem. She proposed to change the earth. After this had been done, the plants began to grow further and further, as splendid as you see before you today.

– So, it was because of the earth? – I honestly show myself astonished.

– That is right, it was infected with some kind of virus, which is why nothing useful could ever have thrived in it. It was never the plants! That's exactly the same thing that happens to most people in network marketing or any other project. Their thinking is paralysed by various viruses, the worst part being that they don't even know it. They do everything they can to change the project, just like I did with the plants, under the illusion that the next one would be better for them. But the new projects do not succeed either, as was the case with the plants. Once you become aware of the need to renew "your earth", it won't matter what you do.

– Okay, but what kind of virus are you talking about exactly?

– One of them we briefly addressed yesterday, namely the virus of acquired and unfounded fears. Other viruses are those of lack of self-confidence, of "what will people say?", of self-pity, of conformism, of victimhood, of ingratitude, of excessive ambition or envy. I could continue the list for a long time, each of us more or less carrying his or her personal collection with him or her, depending on his or her environment of origin. We all bring with us different experiences and imprints that have given room to different kinds of viruses. The worst thing about them is that they multiply each other.

– Yes, you told me yesterday about this infection, but I cannot understand the comparison with viruses. You can cure a virus with various treatments, but the things you are talking about are not.

– In order for a treatment method to be available to you, someone must first have isolated, researched and understood the virus in question. It's the same with the pathogens I'm talking about. Let's walk a little while and talk.

We are choosing a path whose beauty and magic is difficult to put into words. On both sides of the path there are various bushes and flowers lined up, which are so harmoniously matched in colour that they could compete with the most magnificent palace gardens.

– Let me explain it to you differently. Our brain can be compared to a computer, and we should look at it as such. As I have already explained to you, quantum physics comes to this conclusion. During childhood, our parents make every effort to educate us. Unfortunately, in this way, at best, they succeed in installing the same programs for us that they themselves have already stored. A part of the viruses is contained in this "mental software".

– A part? Then where are the rest?

– In the heart, the most dangerous. They emerged from the first viruses, and you could call them "emotional viruses". Our closest loved ones, such as parents and family members or teachers, have to struggle with their own contradictions, their viruses, from their inner world. Influenced by these viruses, they do and say things that cause lifelong emotional blockages in the extremely sensitive children. These in turn lead to countless fears in the little ones, which ultimately create a lack of self-confidence and self-esteem. And in the end, they develop into a shadow of what would have been possible and carry vestigial souls within them.

– My parents did their best.

– I won't deny that, as I have already assured you. What your parents didn't know is that they didn't know anything. Like all fathers and mothers, they thought they knew what they were doing. They all attend courses and workshops to learn a thousand different activities, but who takes a course in child rearing? Today there are a few, but certainly no one at the time when you were a child. I can't stand parents shouting at their children, thinking they speak the same language. But the fact is that children speak a different language than adults. Parents love their children, but out of ignorance, they end up infecting their sensitive brains and hearts and loading them with all their emotional baggage.

– I know what you mean, and I can relate to it. When I was a child, my parents fought a lot, and I suffered in silence. In many significant moments of my life, I also missed a little more confidence on their part in me.

– Don't feel bad, it happened to most of us. If we don't properly understand that they themselves have been programmed by others and don't forgive them, we fire the virus of victimhood. Many people carry this infection within them for life, it is widespread. We blame everything and everyone but ourselves for our shortcomings. This is another serious mistake that this "deceitful software" brings us to, namely the lack of responsibility. My dear, you are one hundred percent responsible for your own life. That is the naked truth. You will only develop further when you stop blaming others. Only when you stop blaming others will you move forward.

– But according to you, they're the ones who infected me.

– Since they didn't know, you can't blame them. As you saw for yourself, they did their best. There is no doubt about that.

Very well, then, how can I disinfect myself? How do I do that?

– As I said, for starters, forgive everyone and everything, including your parents, teachers, friends, etc. And more importantly, forgive yourself, and also your past. People carry all sorts of guilt from the past that robs them of all energy and makes them unable to make new decisions.

– Understood, that sounds very simple at first. But what you are describing is quite difficult.

– It is only difficult because you have not yet understood. Don't worry, that will come. The question is simple: Do you wish for a different life, based on new and own decisions, which will allow you to live a fulfilled life? Or do you prefer to remain stuck in your past and blame everyone for your misfortune? You, and you alone, have a choice. It is essential to learn how to forgive and forgive yourself. Only you can do it, no one can help you. Once you have learned to forgive, you will realise how crucial this ability is for a healthy life. You will ask yourself why you did not start forgiving earlier.

— Can this be compared to resetting a computer?

— Very good, you're about to catch it. After resetting, however, you will need to install new, virus-free programs, with content adapted to who you are and want to be. As the name of Step One, "Learning to Learn," says, this is how you develop into a better version of yourself every day.

Suddenly, Joe leaves the path and after a few quick steps, stands next to a tree that rises a few meters away.

— Another causality link, Jorge! Come and watch the branch of this tree!

A bit more clumsy than Joe I fight my way through the bushes and try not to damage them. Nevertheless, I step on a small patch of wildflowers and finally reach the branch in question.

— Causality? No matter how hard I try, I only see the branch of a tree. What are you talking about?

— I told you to watch it, not just look at it.

So, I go a little closer and I see something green on the branch, different in colour from the rest of it, dangling down at the height of my chest. From Joe's look I conclude that he was talking about it. I pull the glasses out of the breast pocket of my shirt to see better.

— You mean that one? — I point to the green something — It looks like a bean. I don't know what it is.

— It's funny, nature has always been my greatest teacher, along with Don José. She has lessons for all situations, including business. Now she is offering us her support once again. You are facing one of the greatest lessons she has given me in all these years. It's been a long time since I've seen one.

— None what? What is it? — Joe keeps coming up with these riddles.

– You have before you a puppet, my friend, the great lesson of real transformation. In the old days, she was a caterpillar who, when the time came, decided to follow her instincts. Surely, she too felt fear, just as you did on the plane. Undoubtedly, she did not really know what to do, nor how to do it. But she did, or rather she is doing it right now. In the same way, we human beings have to recognise the right moment for our inner metamorphosis and give our spirit new wings. Just like the mythical bird Phoenix, it is up to us to rise anew from our ashes. Most people seek their happiness by doing the same as twenty or thirty years ago. However, they themselves are no longer the same, which means that they should adapt their goals and ways of life. They are so busy with bare survival that they don't even think about it. They never choose a time to hatch out of the cocoon, shed their skin and spread their wings. Like caterpillars, they drag themselves behind a fixed contract of employment to pay their bills. And what about you, Jorge? Are you ready for your metamorphosis?

– To turn me into a butterfly? – I'm joking.

– No – he's looking me straight in the eye. – Rather, to become the best version of yourself that you never dreamed possible. And this is no joke, but probably the most serious and important decision of your life.

– Sorry, I didn't mean to be superficial. Of course, I want a real change in my life, Joe. I'm tired of living to pay bills – do I tell him in a husky voice because I've actually been slaving away for the last few years and I'm sick of this situation.

– Don't worry, Jorge, nothing happens without a reason. We have to get to work now, that's the important thing. I don't want to appear too harsh, but all this is extremely important, so I wish you would understand it very well. This is one of the most crucial decisions of your life. It requires you to abide forever by every single point of the agreement you have signed. You will also have to make an effort to bring about change. Changes are usually associated with pain. But the point is that in the long run it will be much more painful not to bring about these changes.

– I suppose the caterpillar also hurts when its wings grow – really slowly I'm beginning to see the light.

– The process may not be pleasant, but the caterpillar decides not to drag itself along. It makes the decision to venture into the unknown in order to change. There is no guarantee for it, but it is not deterred. Nor has she attended a course in which she was taught how to become a butterfly. But she knows she can be more than a caterpillar, the best version of herself she once dreamed of, a butterfly who can show everyone her true potential.

We watch the cocoon attentively. Never before have I realised what a miracle this natural phenomenon is. The lesson to be learned from this is truly incredible.

– If you don't do your best to bring about a real change, your personal transformation will never become a reality. Without it, you may be able to generate extra income to make ends meet, but you won't reach your true goal, which is freedom. And this is where one of the points of your agreement comes into play, namely that you must be relentless honest with yourself, Jorge.

– Isn't it enough just to be honest? That "relentless" sounds a bit harsh, doesn't it?

– Ha-ha-ha! I'm sorry if it seems that way, but there's no more appropriate way to put it. Trying to be more or less sincere isn't enough. I am talking about something else, namely that form of honesty that makes you cry, that makes you decide to stop pretending and realise that your days on this planet are very limited. You should realise that you only have one chance to live and you must not let it pass by unused. I mean, you should remember your biggest dreams and do everything to make them come true. Delete survival mode and install the program that lets you fight for the life of your dreams. I'm talking about spreading your wings to bestow your most precious gifts upon yourself and the world. But let me tell you this, my friend, without this unsparing honesty you will never be able to make the decision that will change your life and the lives of those you love. Without it, you will not be able to give up certain things that keep you stuck, and in return do others that will guide you to your new life. But as I told you before, everything has a price. Change does not come for free, but the problem is that without it, you pay a lot more. It's about taking the third point of the agreement seriously, which is to be ruthlessly honest with yourself. Over the years, I have noticed how people are constantly deluding themselves. They want to achieve something, but their actions lead in the opposite direction to their wishes. When I was alcoholic, I wanted things to go well in my jobs. I wished for that with a great deal of longing. However, at the slightest setback my brain began to sabotage me until I showed my pessimistic and negative behaviour again. And already I had got the next bottle of whisky. What I lacked was inner strength, which made me cowardly and unstable. The worst thing was that the more I drank, the worse I felt. Thanks to Don José's advice and tasks I was able to strengthen my self-confidence considerably and almost got rid of alcohol by myself. Remember, one of the viruses I told you about is a lack of self-confidence. Only one step away from this is depression. Many people stuff themselves full of antidepressants because they have not succeeded and they have not decided to reshape their lives and dreams. As a result, life weighs heavily on their shoulders. Like a caterpillar, they drag themselves along until they finally die and disappear.

Joe's descriptions get closer and closer to me, I recognise myself one hundred percent in his words. The dreams of new projects I had years ago are dead to me. Lately I have even started to take a sleeping pill every now and then. The truth is that I have not been able to move forward or backward in my life for a long time. Or I do, when I argue with Sara, I slip down a little more. Ever since we bought the house, everything seems to revolve around paying off the mortgage. The debt has severely damaged our relationship. We hardly ever travel, don't go out for dinner, and the highest of feelings we allow ourselves is to go to the movies on Saturday afternoons. Even our desire to have children has vanished into thin air for fear of new expenses due to a baby.

– By the way, I forgot to ask, how did Sara take it that I kidnapped you for two days?

– Well, you know... – he seems to have read my mind. I'm beginning to think that Joe is telepathically predisposed.

– What do I know? – he enquires.

– Not really well, I left her pretty upset this morning. Sunday dinner with her family means a lot to her.

– Don't worry, she'll understand when her life changes for the better because of your new priorities. You have to be careful, because before you know it, you will be caught up in the priorities of those close to you. Family, partners, children or friends often become, without you realising it, great robbers of our time. According to their will, we should go to places at certain times or do things that run counter to our dreams and desires. By this I do not mean that you should not have a good relationship with all of them. Of course, you should, it's incredibly important. What is important is a balance between the time you devote to work and the time you devote to your loved ones. Family and friends are very important, so you have to do everything you can to gain the necessary freedom to enjoy "Quality time" with them. Never forget that quality comes before quantity. I just mean you have to set priorities. In the first place, you have to put your own life and your dreams. This does not mean being selfish, but taking responsibility for your life, which is something completely different. As I can predict, you will not be able to eat with your in-laws or sleep out on Sundays for a while. Dreams do not know weekends, habits or parents in-laws. Remember in these moments that one day they will understand you and be very proud of you. Setting priorities is one of the prizes to be accepted.

– I understand that, Joe, but sometimes it's not so easy.

– Did I say it would be easy? Nothing worth fighting for is easy, but always involves effort. Sometimes it's not just physical effort, but emotional effort as well. Do you remember the Book of Signs by Paulo Coelho that you told me about?

– The Alchemist?

– Do you know why the alchemists were so famous?

– Because they turned lead into gold, or at least claimed to do so – I answer like a shot from a gun.

– Yes, exactly! So, you could say that I will try to make you an alchemist of yourself and therefore of your business.

– Me an alchemist? I don't understand you, Joe.

– Symbolically turning lead into gold can be applied to many facets of our lives. My conviction goes so far that the alchemists of old used to refer to this very inner transformation. Lead stands for the old and gold for the new. The caterpillar that laboriously drags itself along is lead, the butterfly that flutters through the air is gold. By the way, I think now is the right time to tell me about your experiences of the last few months in your network marketing project.

– All right, well... – ... this is the moment I was dreading. As you can probably already imagine, it didn't go very well. I came across it through a neighbour who told me about it at a barbecue. At first, I was enthusiastic. It seemed perfect. I assumed that all my friends would go into business with me and see things as clearly as I did. To be on the safe side, I ordered thirty contracts and was totally enthusiastic. And so, I started to go through my contact list and my first disappointment followed. Many people let me down, either didn't even want to come to the presentation to listen to it or didn't have time. Others warned me that I would be cheated, and there was even someone who informed others of my impending call and questioned the feasibility of the deal. I don't need to mention that I was quite distant from this person and I am a little angry with others as well. You have disappointed me.

– Don't worry, the time will come when they will understand you. It's very important not to be angry with anyone. It happens more often than you think. Very soon you'll see things in a more positive and constructive light. You'll have presented the business to some people, right?

– Yeah, sure, about a dozen people, I guess.

– And what happened to it?

– Well, only two friends went into business, but they don't show much ambition. Honestly, the day of the accident, I wanted to quit.

– Luckily, I landed on you, ha, ha, ha ...

His laughter is getting really on my nerves, and this time I have a great desire to give Joe a fist punch. How can he laugh at my situation?

– No offence, but he's reading my mind again. It's just that so many are experiencing the same thing, and you're no exception. You're probably just going about it the wrong way, but that's not the problem. It's just about understanding certain things and doing them in a more intelligent way. You don't know it yet, but to start like this is a blessing.

– A blessing? That's great – I say sourly.

– Ha, ha, ha ... Don't get upset. Once you learn to use alchemy in business, everything will be crystal clear for you. However, you should understand that all worthwhile projects require development, which in certain moments may seem like defeat. Mind you, I did use the word "seemingly". Do you know the saying that "All that glitters is not gold"?

– Of course, I do.

– Don José used as wise a pun as the original saying when I suffered these small setbacks. "Not everything that doesn't shine is lead," he told me in such situations with a firm look. I can literally see him in front of me. Indeed, the fear of failure is one of the worst viruses. But I want to tell you one of the most important things you will hear in your whole life: Defeat leads you directly to success!

– What? Are you kidding me, Joe?

– I never joke about these things. In fact, Don José wanted me to set myself negative defeat goals, not monthly success goals. I want you to do the same. Only by increasing your number of defeats can you increase your chances of success. You cannot imagine how many negative experiences I have had over the years, mainly at the beginning of course. But they could not destroy my dreams, because I had understood what they really were, namely unavoidable small steps towards my freedom. I am aware that this may sound a bit strange, but in network marketing as well as in life, defeats are real teachers and friends.

They form the core of your personal story of self-development, which will lead you to the peak of success. I know people, including myself, who have told their own story of self-development countless times. It moves others who can recognise and identify with it. This story teaches them that if I have been able to overcome all obstacles, they too will be able to do so. Personal stories have the power to change lives. And remember, your personal story began long before you signed a contract with your network marketing company. Value the bad start as a gift, because that's all it is. A resource that, when well used, will prove to be an ideal partner on your path of personal growth. Without obstacles to overcome, there is no positive success story. We will take the wind out of your worst fears to make them your strongest allies. Are you beginning to understand why I told you that you would become an expert in alchemy?

– When you put it that way, it makes sense. But what do you think about all the stupid things I have to listen to inside and outside the family?

– What stupidities are you referring to?

– That I'm being cheated on, that it's not for me, that I should spend time with her...

– Ha-ha-ha! It's all part of the game, don't take it seriously. We've all lived through it. All the great inventors and geniuses were considered crazy at the time. Let's get back to alchemy. Everything you're telling me clearly indicates that you're doing something that's really worth doing. Take a look at their lives. I assume they are neither successful entrepreneurs nor inventors, nor do they do anything else that could initiate a definitely necessary change in their lives. Write this down well in your notebook, Jorge. As I told you, my system is only two steps, but there are the "Eight Fatal Traps of Network Marketing", as I call them.

– Gee, the word "fatal" sounds pretty extreme, doesn't it?

– We need clear language, so the word "fatal" does not come out of nowhere. Every one of these traps you fall into will definitely dampen and slow down your business significantly, but most of the time such a mistake even means the definitive end. I can tell you this for sure, because I have observed it hundreds of times. These are traps that many people fall into without realising it, and afterwards they cannot explain it. In the end, they give up and believe that this business does not work.

– Well then, please tell me.

– I'd like to do that: The First Fatal Trap is "Let Dream Killers Guide You".

– What the hell are dream killers?

– Often, some or even many of our friends and family members do not trust our new project, which is why our dream of success and freedom is easily endangered by their unqualified opinions. It is wrong to put your life in the hands of others' opinions, otherwise you will end up like them.

You know, Jorge, over all these years I have met many people and have found that there are countless "commentators" but far fewer "doers". The former are conformists with modest dreams, if they still have any. In contrast, the second group do have dreams, big dreams, and they fight for them. When they fall, they don't give in, but straighten up again and try again. It is better to pay little attention to the "commentators", but if a "doer" speaks to you, listen to him carefully, because he can always teach you something. Recently, scientists have discovered the so-called "mirror neurons", which unconsciously imitate the actions and feelings of the people around us. So, you have the choice: Who do you want to resemble?

– You are right, of course. I would really like to contradict you, but I can't. But with Sara or my family, things are more complicated.

– It's a little more delicate between the couple and the family. Here it's up to you to be patient and have personal conviction about your project. But don't worry, because as soon as Sara and your family see concrete results that will improve their lives, and notice how you as a person are also developing positively overall, they will understand and support you. In fact, they will become your biggest fans. Remember, I told you that for a real change in your life, you need to learn how to relate to others from the ground up. This includes your family and Sara. To give true love, you must also learn to love yourself first.

While Joe clears some stones from the side of the road, I think about what I should think about this. When he has finished, he interrupts my thoughts.

– You seem very thoughtful, Jorge.

– Yeah, all this really makes me think. On the one hand you are right, and I have to do everything I can to fight for a better life, but on the other hand I am stressed that there are seven more fatal traps waiting for me.

– Don't worry, it's not just traps coming. I have good news for you. Follow me!

The Lever

We branch off onto another path to a nearby shed. A few meters before the entrance we stop and Joe points to a large stone with a challenging gesture.

– Try to lift it a little.

– What? It's gotta weigh more than 30 kilos. I'm still in pain from the accident. Should I go back to the hospital for a few days? – I object slightly irritated at his unreasonable idea.

– Would you like to know how you can lift it up despite pain and without going to hospital? – he disappears into the shed and shortly afterwards steps out again with an iron bar and a piece of wood. – Do you know what that is? – he wants to know when he puts the objects beside the stone.

– An iron bar and a piece of wood.

– Ha-ha-ha! It's not just any iron bar. Look at the shape of it. It's a lever. And the piece of wood will serve as a support. Remember Archimedes´ words: "Give me a fixed point, and I will unhinge the world. " I'm not asking that much of you, but can you lift the stone a few inches?

– Okay, I don't know what you're getting at, but I'll give it a shot. But we're gonna stop as soon as it hurts, all right?

– Sure, so go ahead.

I reach for the lever that Joe put down with the piece of wood as the fulcrum before. I try to adopt a position that is as painless as possible, press the lever down, and to my amazement the heavy stone goes up a few inches almost without effort. I had never used a lever before, and I am honestly amazed because of the increased strength.

– You are probably wondering why I let you move a stone.

– I would really like to know that.

– Well, I told you I wanted to bring you good news. Besides the "Eight Fatal Traps" I will also give you the "Eight Magic Levers of Network Marketing". And of course, I provide you with the appropriate fulcrum, without which the levers won't work. A lever is quite simply a tool that potentiates and optimises your efforts, just like the "Magic Levers" that I would like to introduce to you.

– Please tell me the first one.

– Gladly. The first lever seems to be the opposite of the first trap, but it is more subtle and says: "Leverage yourself out of your opponents. Use their lack of faith in you to increase your power and prove to them what you are capable of. Would they dare to jump out of a plane without warning if they suffer from fear of heights? I doubt it. I have seen many extremely successful people whose greatest motivation for perseverance was precisely that. Think to yourself: "You don't believe in me? I will show you what I am made of. You will meet the real Jorge and see where I can go. "

When you lever yourself out of your opponents, you will always have an energy advantage. Alchemy, my friend, pure alchemy.

– You love to twist and turn everything completely until you find a positive angle. Until now I couldn't see things the way you explain them to me. You literally turn lead into gold. In truth, I'd like to prove to everyone how much more I'm capable of than they give me credit for. I realise I have much more to give, and I'm angry that they didn't see that. That would make me feel wonderful.

– Then pull the lever on that anger! Use it to your advantage and you become an alchemist! But above all, you must try to understand. That way you will be able to take one decisive step after the other. And by understanding, I mean both the brain in your head and the brain in your heart. This means that you should understand and feel it at the same time. Scientists have found out that our heart consists of 65% nerve cells and not muscle cells. Did you know that? Some even believe that the heart controls the brain and not the other way around. We also think with the heart, my friend. And remember, the language of the heart is feelings, not words. So, let that anger work its magic to give you the strength you need.

After I write the last notes in my book, I think about it. Joe has a strange way of turning things around, becoming an alchemist, as he puts it. It makes sense, though, and he really stirs me up. I realise how much I've lost or had contact with life. I'm about to turn into a shadow of my former self. I can't even remember my dreams. It can't go on like this, I have to take the leap. It's time to get to work.

– Fine, but how do I do it to make my business work? I attend all the meetings and workshops, have read who knows how many books on the subject, but when the going gets tough, those invited say goodbye without signing a contract. Besides, I hardly have any contacts left to recruit.

– First of all, you have to create a successful Step One. Only when you have at least a dozen people who take things reasonably seriously and join your business directly, thereby reaching the upper levels, is this crucial Step One completed. Step One is the most important, in my opinion much more important than Step Two. It lays the foundation on which you can build your business. And as you know, the quality of the bricks or windows is of no use without a good foundation, because no matter what you build on it, sooner or later it will become brittle. So, you can imagine that you will have to present the business to many people. Because how should it be possible to realise financial freedom and your dream life if you only present it to your family and a few friends? That doesn't make much sense, this approach lacks any common sense. Let me give you an example to illustrate: Imagine that tomorrow you are preparing to launch a new clothing brand in your country exclusively. The quality is very high at very attractive prices, but nobody knows about it yet. Surely you would sell the first clothes to your family, right?

– I suppose so, yes.

– But do you think the project would be very successful only by selling to your inner circle?

– Of course not, I'd have to find shops to resell the clothes.

– Do you think that the owners of these shops would visit you at home to buy your clothes without knowing of your existence?

– Of course not, Joe. I don't have any stores to offer my network marketing business to, though.

– No, you have it much easier because you need people instead of business. And from what I understand, there are a lot more people than shops. The whole city is filled with people! If there's one thing that's really crowded, it's this!

– That's true, but I don't know most of them. I'm a bit shy and have difficulty approaching strangers. It seems like I'm selling them something.

– The crucial question in this case is: What price are you willing to pay? Is it too high a price for your freedom to overcome the fear of getting in contact with little-known or completely unknown people? If so, we'd better put an end to all this and you'll seek refuge behind the mountains of paper at your desk. Remember what we talked about fears. Don't be put off, Jorge, don't allow it. Shame and shyness form a wall that keeps us away from life and are part of the psychological viruses that we need to eradicate as soon as possible.

You must also examine your own concept of the business, of your products and of yourself. If you were deeply convinced of the high value of your offer for everyone, it would be easy for you to promote it. The problem is that you don't believe in your business or yourself at the moment. Furthermore, I would not call it selling, but recommending products that could change people's lives for the better. You are also offering them the opportunity to work with you and a team, backed by your energetic support in building a thriving business. Your offer enables them to improve their lives in many ways with little economic investment. After the business presentation, they will decide whether or not to embark on a transformation of their lives. The decision is ultimately up to them and no longer up to you. But as you know, your business does not depend on their response, but on your constant work. A possible refusal cannot harm you, for you will be immune to their darker side. However, you must improve your conscious and unconscious opinion of your offer, including yourself. We will manage that in these days, don't worry. Actually, I know you are already on the right track.

– To be honest, I had a terrible idea about network marketing yesterday, but your approaches are about to change everything. However, I do have a practical question: what do I do with people who tell me after the business presentation that they have to try the products for a few months before they start, and then disappear from the scene? I've seen several of them.

– Excuses, my dear, these are excuses not to have to face their fears. You must learn to distinguish between excuses and real doubt. Unfortunately, "excuses" is another psychological virus common among humans. Put these people to the test and ask them how long it would take them to sign the contract if, instead of a direct marketing system, your company offered a non-terminable contract with a monthly salary of €10,000 plus two months' vacation per year. Surely, they wouldn't hesitate that long and have to test the products, what do you think?

– Definitely not. I suppose they would sign as soon as possible so as not to let the opportunity pass. That's a great question. I'd like to ask them, see how they react. You're absolutely right, they are excuses. But what about those who tell me they don't like anything to do with sales. Is that another excuse?

– Yeah, offer them the 10,000 Euro contract, and you'll see how quickly they'd get excited. As I said, I never thought of it as selling anything, but as providing valuable information that could improve people's lives. I don't know if you've realised it, but in this society, everybody sells something, including you.

– Well, you're wrong. In my job as an accountant, I'm not selling anything.

– Ha-ha-ha! Serious mistake, my friend. You also sell day after day, only it is not the hypothetical branded clothes or any other product, but much worse, you sell your time, your life and your dreams for a salary. But since it is used to pay the bills and to go to the cinema on Saturdays, it seems sufficient to you. The result is a bad deal, certainly the worst deal you can make in your life. Besides, I can't imagine the feeling of spending almost a third of my life in a job that I don't like and where the only ambition is to reach the end of the month alive to collect the salary and check off another month. Moreover, at your age you start every day with the fear of being fired. At my age, and this is considerable, people are fully aware of the importance of quality of life, and the necessary steps that must be taken to achieve this. As I said, the greatest risk is not to take any risks.

– Well, if I do my job well, they have no reason to fire me.

– Maybe not, but they might. That decision is not up to you, and you will always be dependent on your boss' decisions. A bad business decision can bankrupt any company, and your job can be gone. Or a relative of your boss may become unemployed and need a job in the company. This means that your work and salary depend on numerous factors, of which you have almost no control over. That is, if your job has existed this long.

– My job is to disappear? I don't think so, accountants will always be needed.

– Ha-ha-ha! Don't you realise that the fourth industrial revolution is already underway?

– The fourth? I thought the digital revolution was the third...

– You're right, the digital revolution with PCs, mobile phones and the Internet as protagonists was the third. But now we are already at the beginning of the fourth, the revolution in artificial intelligence and robotics.

– And what does that have to do with my work?

– Well, in ten years' time your accountant job will probably be taken over by a robot, and much better and faster than you can do it. Not only accountants, the most competent experts in this field worldwide predict that by 2030, 50% of the professions known today will disappear globally and be taken over by robots that do not complain, do not eat, do not sleep and do not fall ill. In the labour market, the most radical change in history is imminent. Everything is being automated by means of cyber-physical systems, as scientists call them. The more mechanical your work is, the more likely you are to be replaced by a robot. This is true of your profession, as it is of many others. That alone should make you aware that the term "safe job" has become practically obsolete. Find out for yourself and you will see that I am not exaggerating in the slightest.

– You're beginning to depress me... – I reply a little sadly.

– Have you already forgotten the alchemy? Try again to see the gold in the lead. The good news is that all these people are going to need something to do, and I'm sure your network marketing business will be a great opportunity for them. After all, these business models flourish especially in times of employment crises.

– You think our business will be spared from automation?

– I am convinced of that.

Silently, we walk back a bit while I take in Joe's arguments. In the distance, I see the lake from yesterday, which we seem to be heading for. The chirping of birds and crickets underscore the peaceful atmosphere of this little paradise. As we approach the lake, I recognise a fisherman, apparently the same as yesterday, checking his fishing rod.

– Look, there's Manuel! He's a friendly neighbour who loves fishing here. He stands there for hours with his rod, always with a smile on his face. Come, we'll talk to him – quietly we walk towards him until Joe breaks the silence with his deep voice. Hello, Manuel! Look, I want you to meet a good friend of mine. His name is Jorge.

– Hello, Joe! How are you, Jorge? I'm glad to meet you. If you're a good friend of Joe's, you're a friend of mine too.

– Pleased to meet you, Manuel. Likewise – I say politely – how are you?

– Very well, as usual. I caught a few beauties today.

– You can say that again – Joe notices with a glance at the basket next to Manuel. There will be fish at your place tonight.

After a few minutes of animated conversation, a pleasant silence is created, where we can listen to the sounds of nature. Joe pulls a strange face, then his penetrating voice sounds again.

– Manuel, may I ask you something? How many times did you cast your fishing line this morning?

– I don't know, Joe. Maybe a hundred or a hundred and fifty times? I really don't know, Joe, I haven't kept count.

– Excellent answer, Manuel, thank you very much. We must go now, and we do not want to disturb your triumph and peace any longer. Give my regards to your wife.

– Goodbye, Joe, and thanks for letting me enjoy this wonderful place.

We turn back and let Manuel continue fishing undisturbed. After a few meters, Joe stops and looks at me as if he wants to tell me something important.

– Did you hear? A hundred and fifty times. What do you think would happen if Manuel would give up on the sixth or seventh try with an empty fishing hook?

– Well, I suppose he couldn't bring anything home for dinner.

– Exactly! It's the same in business, but Manuel has a distinct advantage.

– What's that? – I ask curiously.

– He takes into account every futile attempt, he knows that from the very beginning. He also knows that every empty fishing hook brings him closer to the next catch. When recruiting you have to adopt this attitude. Don José always said that the "right attitude" would enable me to really enjoy the business. He said that if I didn't like what I was doing, including the acquisition, I wouldn't have understood. This means that if you know from the start that there will be setbacks, you will even like them over time instead of allowing them to knock you down. Remember we talked about your personal history. All these failures are inscribed in your story, and overcoming these small and apparent failures is necessary so that in the future you can stand by those who find themselves in similar situations and turn to you for inspiration and motivation. You should learn to enjoy and appreciate setbacks. You must cross this valley if you want to reach the summit of success. The trick is not to take them personally. After all, what some reject is the business, not you. What it's really about is understanding that not everyone has the stuff or the courage to start a business. They will give you countless excuses to say no, but in fact it is their fears that make them feel bad. It is part of business to understand that this will happen more often than you would like. But don't worry about it, because many of them will come to you as soon as you achieve tangible results and they see your success. Always remember the seventh point of the agreement you signed: Patience, you need a lot of patience, my friend. With effort, everything will get going. Your business does not depend on them or anyone else, but only on you. Your job is to sow day after day and to have patience. Every seed needs time to sprout. Make the setbacks your friends. What if one day I visit you at home and you offer me a cup of fine coffee that someone brought from Colombia especially for you, and I tell you I don't like coffee? Would you be mad at me?

– No, Joe, why would I be mad at you about something like that?

– I mean, there's not that much difference. You offer something, and people go along with it and try it or don't try it. It's as simple as that.

– It almost sounds like fun when you put it that way.

– From the right perspective, anger at failure actually seems funny. But before we go any further, I'll tell you a little trick that has always helped me. Don José instructed me to write a few sentences in my notebook and read them several times immediately after a rejection. You should feel them even more than you read them. I remember very well the countless times I went through them. So, write it down.

> *"I'm a winner and I pursue my dreams.*
> *No obstacle will deter me from my goal.*
> *I like rejection because it makes me stronger and wiser.*
> *I appreciate setbacks because they shape my personal history.*
> *My story is my best partner on the way to the summit.*
> *Thank you, dear obstacles, for forming my character."*

– Repeat the sentences over and over again and feel their meaning, just as I did in all those years after rejections, and you will realise the power of these words. Always carry the phrase with you and do not underestimate this tool. The most effective things are often the seemingly simplest. It is important to always remember to read and feel it after every setback of any kind. The effect unfolds not only in business matters, but in every negative situation in life.

– I think this is a great idea. The words are very inspiring and wise. Besides, in such moments everything else does not offer much help either.

– Not much help? Then keep writing, because now comes the Second Magic Lever, "The Power of Probabilities". It sounds silly but calculating with probabilities is pure alchemy. You just have to use your average values. For example, if one person out of every ten people you approach about the business finally gets it, your average success rate is 10%, which is brilliant.

– You call 10% genius? It seems anything but genius to me.

– Well, Manuel thought less than 1.5% success was genius.

– Come on, it doesn't compare.

– The important thing is to know one fundamental factor from the outset, namely to know about the nine upcoming rejections before a new partner joins. That way, you can count on it, which gives you a completely new perspective. If you don't want any refusals, you have to go back to your accountant's desk to make your boss' dreams come true. At the expense of your own, of course.

– No, please don't. I want out of this office.

– Then take things to heart. Instead of setting performance targets, we'll do as Don José did with me. From now on, you'll set weekly and monthly cancellation targets, failure targets. That will be your first priority. What do you think is the beginning of fifteen cancellations a week?

– Fifteen? Isn't that a little high?

– Too high-minded, you mean? Don José told me to aim for thirty a week at the beginning. But I think fifteen is enough for a start, that's two a day. What are you complaining about? To contact a potential partner takes maybe five minutes, multiplied by two, that's ten minutes' net per day. Does that seem like a lot of work?

– Well, you have to factor in the time it takes me to show them the business at my place.

– Have you successfully introduced the business to your contacts without the presence of your uplines? – he objects with a clearly negative gesture.

– Yes, of course, I did the presentations at my home, except once, when we went to the central meeting.

– You have made a bad mistake, my friend. You have fallen into the Second Fatal Trap and have almost caused your business to fail. As I warned you, the traps are really deadly.

– What does it consist of? – Because I'm so engrossed in the conversation, I didn't even notice that we're almost back at the house again. Joe goes to a garage and opens the door.

– Come on in, I'll show you. – You're gonna show me the trap?

– That's right.

We enter the garage, where it smells of a mixture of paint, wood and iron, and lots of tools are lined up in impeccable order. We walk towards something covered with a big tarp. Joe points me out to help him. When the two of us have removed the tarpaulin, I see a wonderful old-timer car, polished to a high gloss, in perfect condition.

– You like it?

– Yes, it's incredibly beautiful.

– I found it in a junkyard and I restored it bit by bit. I am very happy with the result. As you can see, alchemy is possible with almost anything. Mary and I love to take it out on sunny days. Get in on the driver's side.

As I take my seat in the driver's seat, I see what a great job Joe has done. The car is a beauty and well maintained in every detail.

– It is beautiful, but what does the car have to do with the trap?

– Start it up and you'll see! – I start the engine, it purrs like a kitten.

– If you wanted to take a drive, which gear would you put in?

– Obviously the first, do you think I'm stupid?

– No, Jorge, don't get upset. What if instead of first gear, you tried fourth? Go ahead, try it.

– I don't even have to try, Joe. I'd stall the engine, and it wouldn't start. That's obvious.

– Yes, with a system like an engine, that's pretty obvious, but why doesn't it apply to a system like network marketing?

– What do you mean?

– Everything has its order, and if you change it, most of the time it won't work out well.

– Order? So, where's the trap?

– The trap is "try to put step two before step one". This is fatal. I'm surprised how many people do the same thing. In my method, you don't even present your business directly until step two. Like countless others, you have not understood the importance of teamwork and the goal-oriented use of the network marketing system. Every system consists of stages in a certain order, don't forget that. Network marketing, like the gears of engines, is a system of stages. If you skip some, it just won't work well. Step one is simply to go to as many events as possible and get people to attend business presentations where a person with already tangible results and therefore more experience than you can share their success story. If you go to a central meeting, you are on the safe side, because the person presenting the business there will undoubtedly have results. However, if you are organising a presentation at your home, you should preferably have a leader from your sponsor line do the talking. They will be happy to support you in your efforts to motivate people. Remember that it is their team and their business. There is usually no shortage of uplines with a proven track record of success who are willing to help and get involved. What's usually lacking is salespeople who can persuade others to do a great job of completing Step One. As you also know, practice makes perfect. Skilfully completing Step One makes you an expert at getting people to move and recruit potential partners. Being really good at something feels wonderful because you can pass on your knowledge from experience, not theoretically or by necessity. If you are able to teach many people how to accomplish Step One, you are sure to succeed. It is as simple as that. Later I will tell you about Step Two, but I will tell you now, in very simple terms, that the most successful network marketers have come this far because they have gotten many members of their organisation to complete a first-class Step One and reach the upper levels. No more, no less, my friend.

– Fair enough, but I don't like the way they present the business, and I don't like some of them.

– You think you can do better on your own?

– Well, it seems more trustworthy to me, and the atmosphere during the presentation is more relaxed.

– A presentation is not there to relax, but to work. And I have some bad news for you: Your words don't really carry any weight yet, nor any value in terms of business. I am sorry to have to tell you this, with commitment and perseverance this will change. But for now, it's a fact. They will gain weight as you gradually expand your personal story, building on experience, obstacles overcome and results achieved. At this point, you can then move on to Step Two, based on a solid business and experience base. In Step One you build the foundation of your business, and you know what happens to a house without a solid foundation. In summary, a presentation should simply never take place without someone with a personal track record recommending the system that got them this far. Don't worry, I am absolutely convinced that you will soon be giving masterful presentations yourself. But you're in the early stages, where you need a lot of support from your team. You should also attend as many presentations as possible so that you can learn different styles and find your own. Some you will like better than others, and some partners you will like more than others, but don't be foolish enough to judge them hastily. If they have a success story to offer, their words will always carry more weight than yours in this initial phase. When they talk about income, it is tangible because they are already earning well. They will talk about their personal history, their lived experience. You, however, earn little or hardly anything at all, and you lack experience. So how do you want to talk about earnings or other prospects? The system is based on good teamwork. Let the uplines introduce the business in step one. Would you jump in a parachute with someone you know has only jumped twice in his life? Or would you rather jump in a parachute with someone who's had a thousand jumps in his life like me? Delegate this part to the team and for now concentrate on encouraging people to attend the presentations. What do you think would happen in your company if the warehouse helper were to take the place of the general manager or vice versa?

– Knowing her, it would probably cause a real disaster.

– "Learning to learn" also implies learning how to delegate different tasks to the most qualified people. In the beginning, your ego, infected by the damn viruses, will put a damper on your learning, because it always wants to be the centre of attention. But for good teamwork you need a lot of modesty. I also advise you to never lose this attitude, because it will make your way much more fruitful and productive. Your greatest asset in business and in life is to cultivate humility. It will prevent you from falling into the second fatal trap. Moreover, you will miss the power of the "Third Magic Lever" if you go about everything on your own as before.

– The third lever? – I am writing in my book as we get out of the car.

– Take this chair. Let's enjoy the sun until Mary calls us to dinner. I think it will be ready soon. Before we do, there's something I want to show you.

We take two old but sturdy chairs and go to the garage entrance. I notice that Joe is taking an axe, which is by the door. We sit down and after a few moments of silence he continues.

– In order to really understand the third lever, I would like us to first think about the meaning of the words. As I already told you, you change your life when you change your choice of words. Let me give you an example of this. Tell me what this is for – he asks and points to the axe which is now leaning against his chair.

– The axe? Well, primarily for chopping up logs.

Joe stands up with the axe in his right hand and puts a piece of wood on top of a larger one. Then he splits it into two practically equal parts in a demonstrative expert pose with a short and powerful stroke.

– Exactly! You were right. But the question is, is it useful for other things as well?

– What do you mean by that?

– For example – suddenly the familiar friendly expression on his face changes to that of a mentally ill person. He walks towards me with a raised axe, and everything indicates that he will attack me. I cannot believe it. What if this Joe is a psychopath? I try to swerve to avoid the impending axe blow. The abrupt movement causes me to fall backwards out of my chair.

– Ha-ha-ha! Forgive me, Jorge. It was a joke – I hear him say as I'm getting up and running away in horror. – I didn't mean to startle you, but I got carried away with my theatrics.

– What? It's not funny. I almost had a heart attack.

– I'm so sorry. I'm so sorry. I didn't think you'd be so scared. Please accept my apology.

– OK, I accept. You scared the hell out of me, Joe. I really thought you'd gone crazy.

– All joking aside, do you realise how the same axe I use to split wood to heat the stove could be used to do you great harm? Words are exactly the same as the axe, they can do both good and evil. There are two kinds of words, the spoken ones and the imagined ones, because you think in words of your language. With spoken words, you can do a lot of good or a lot of bad to others. With thought words, speak the thought, we have already seen that you can do all sorts of good or all sorts of bad things to yourself and thus to others. When you reproach someone, you do it with words. If you lie, you do it with words as well. On the other hand, you also express your appreciation for someone in words. To tell Sara that you love her, you do it through words. They have incredible power and like all powerful forces it is advisable to control them, otherwise they might turn against you. Through your words, you can conjure up both heaven and hell. You can instil a person with a lot of confidence, or you can inflict a lifelong trauma. Misused words are like the dark arts'. So, we have no choice but to be extremely careful with what comes out of our mouths. However, it is difficult to speak and listen to us at the same time to explore how we express ourselves, don't you think?

– Yes, of course it's complicated, especially when you're nervous. Sometimes I can't even remember what I said because of all the excitement.

– Then underline the following in your notes: Record your business conversations as often as you can with a tape recorder, that's important. There are no excuses for this anymore, because all mobile phones have this function. Remember that you want to get into a business where you need to learn how to communicate properly and you need a basis for practice. You may have heard this advice before, perhaps even more often, but in my experience few people take it seriously. And I tell you once again, it is an absolutely fundamental point. You will be surprised if you follow my advice. Did you know that actors spend thousands of hours in front of the mirror to improve their expression with face and body?

– I don't know any actors, but something like that has come to my attention.

– Your mirror represents your shot. And by listening to yourself, you will discover your mistakes and make the necessary changes for better linguistic expression. In this business, being a good communicator is fundamental.

– I try, Joe.

– Do it instead of just trying. But let's move on to the third lever. You know, it's very interesting what we do with words without realising it, creating images in the minds of others. Do me a favour, please.

– What?

– Don't think of a white giraffe. – Joe ends a brief moment of silence with the expected question. – What is going through your mind right now, Jorge?

– A giant white giraffe, ha, ha, ha...! – we both burst out laughing.

– I think now we can discuss the third lever, which is one of the most crucial.

– What does it consist of, Joe? Now you've got me curious. – "Harness the power of construction," my dear.

– "Edification"?

– That's right, and you're gonna be wondering what to edify. As I just proved to you with your white giraffe, you will construct or create mental images with your words. Actually, you do this all the time when you speak, but not in a controlled way. Building up is essential and can help you in important matters. It is about always creating a positive and authentic image of someone or something that you convey to others. Always speaking well of your business partners is essential. These words will create a positive image in them and others.

For example, to take your presentations on your own initiative: If you had been able to rely on the cooperation of a person from your sponsor line to present the business, you could have told your contacts about him or her and his or her results and experiences. Through these words, you would have created a professional image with a convincing effect in their brains. The problem is, you cannot edify yourself with words. I personally like the building that was created with modesty, commitment and results. Sometimes you will find it easier when you meet people you have a lot of empathy and admiration for, other times you will have people you find harder to build with because there is not so much empathy. But remember, you still have to do it. Concentrate exclusively on their strengths, of which they certainly possess enough. You are in the same boat and you are rowing in the same direction, and for that reason alone this person deserves your respect and admiration. You should learn to recognise the strengths in all people and to bring them to the fore. All too often, because of some mental virus, we focus too much on the mistakes of others and hardly on their good sides. For great teamwork, to be able to fully exploit the multilevel system, this virus must be defeated. As you see people, they will be sooner or later, science has proven that.

– You're right about that. Recently I read an article about a very interesting experiment with students, to what extent the professor's opinion about them affected their grades.

– I know that, too. It's most illuminating. That means it's up to you to focus on your strengths and get the most out of them.

– I promise you, I will focus exclusively on the strengths of all my partners, even my neighbour.

– Ha, ha, ha ...! That's the right attitude. Use the lever of building also to sincerely acknowledge the efforts and progress of the members of your team whenever you have the opportunity. We humans generally have a deficit of recognition for our successes. Does your boss sometimes express his appreciation for your good work and dedication, or does he limit himself to paying your salary?

– Honestly, not only does he not acknowledge my efforts, but I don't get any thanks for the free overtime.

– Yes, many bosses do not realise how important it is to motivate their employees. Those hours you work without pay actually cost him a lot. An unmotivated employee does the bare essentials and tries to get home quickly. In the end, you end up with an office full of zombies instead of employees. Motivation brings out your best skills and strengths, and the best way to motivate someone is not only to pay them decently, but also to show appreciation for what they do well through words and gestures. Motivation alone won't get you far, but without it you won't get anywhere at all. If you acknowledge the success of your partners, you will get the best out of them. Alchemy, my friend, there is always gold to be found under the layer of lead. You must never forget the lever of building if you want to achieve high success rates in this business and, I think, in life as well.

– I understand, in fact my motivation increases significantly when I get constructive words from my partners with more experience in the business. Encouraging words on a bad day are never wrong.

– Then analyse what effect these words have had on you, so you understand why you should use them as often as possible with others. Soon you will have to motivate many people.

– I will, you can count on it.

– You told me that the contact phase is not going well at all.

– What makes you say that?

– Because building is also the key to this phase.

– The key to making contact? Explain it to me in more detail. Recruiting is the area I master least.

– You're not the only one, Jorge. Probably the biggest challenge for everyone in this business, especially in Step One. How do you approach it?

– Well, I call them or make appointments with them, and although I try to explain as little as possible, they always make me give a brief overview of both the product and the industry.

– A clear mistake.

– Oh, Joe... I gotta tell you something.

– Edification is the best tool to get people to attend the

presentations. You edify the project and the entrepreneurial team that teaches and supports you. You also give them the opportunity to get the information from someone very successful. It's very simple.

– That's all?

– That's it, ha, ha, ha ... Our brain with its viruses complicates everything quite a bit. You just have to create an image in their heads. Don't start explaining what this business is all about to anyone on the subway or to a friend on the phone, even if they ask. You can make two convincing arguments if people ask.

– Name them, please.

– Firstly, because it is information that requires a suitable place, certain tools and the necessary time to understand it properly. You cannot ask a musician to interpret Beethoven's Fifth Symphony crammed into a subway train with a violin missing two strings in two minutes. Either interpret it properly or don't start at all. Period.

– You are absolutely right, I will certainly take that argument.

– Also keep in mind that your words do not carry any real weight at the moment, as I have already explained to you. You do not yet have the experience and results that would give them the credibility they deserve. For now, your only task is to arouse interest, not to present the business. Therefore, the second reason you can give for not having to explain is that you are still in training and cannot present the system with the professionalism it deserves. Inform them that you can organise someone with better qualifications and tangible results. You can claim that you would only cause confusion, and since this has already happened, you have decided not to make the same mistake again. Take yourself out of the game, set up the entrepreneur who will present the business the following day, and name the date and time of the event. Then take out your calendar, write down the person's contact details and let them know that you will call them to confirm the appointment with you because you have been very busy lately. Tell her that if she can't come, someone else will take her place. Edify the team that teaches you to re-target your goals with a booming and accessible business model that is open to everyone, and schedule presentations. Do not try to convince them with arguments or explanations at this stage. This will only create a mess that distracts interested parties. If the person wants to go to the presentation, let them go, and if not, don't. You don't have to worry about that, because as you know and as I have told you several times before, your business does not depend on him or her, but on your conviction and consistency. That means it is entirely in your hands.

– But what if they tell me they won't come if I don't provide more information?

– Then they won't. Not everyone is willing to make their life better, or not right now. When I started to have visible success, I regularly received calls from people who didn't want to listen to my information at the time. Don't worry, they will come. My advice is to call or email all those who do not respond to the first contact once a year. Life has countless twists and turns, and your certain results together with any circumstance in their lives can change their minds. Over time, setbacks can turn into successes. This will happen for sure, never forget that.

– Alchemy, I know. Thank you, Joe. What you say seems obvious, but actually I've been doing everything backwards so far.

– In addition to edifying, there's something else that's extremely important in the delicate phase of contacting potential partners.

– Which is what, Joe?

– Edify yourself.

– What do you mean, edifying yourself? You said I can't use words to edify myself up.

– Well, you don't edify yourself with words.

– OK, but then how?

– By treating your best product as carefully as possible.

– My best product? Oh, you mean myself.

– That's right! As I explained to you, you are your best product, so you have to pay attention to your personal image as well as to your attitude and expression. This is absolutely fundamental. A butterfly has elegant wings, and you should take good care of your new image. Be aware that you are now an entrepreneur at the beginning of his great career and no longer an accountant working overtime without pay. Accounting is just one way of paying the bills for a few months until your business allows you to quit this job for good. Dress and express yourself like a successful entrepreneur from now on and you will progress much faster. This will also give you the extra confidence you need to radiate. Everyone first perceives the ambassador before the embassy. You cannot tell anyone about entrepreneurial success if your clothing and posture do not match the message you are conveying. Ambassador and message have to be coherent. The shots we have discussed will help you make significant progress in this crucial business aspect. Full confidence in yourself and your project, coupled with a professional image, will be your best allies in these crucial phases. If you do not follow this advice, you run the risk of becoming your worst product and the worst enemy of your business. Remember, you don't get a second chance at a first impression. Besides, you are representing something!

– What's that supposed to mean?

– You have a good figure and you will look good in a smart suit.

– Ahem...! Joe, I'm a married man – I guess my joke is a little risqué.

– What? Some joker – he's trying to give me a slap on the back of the neck I can barely dodge – Ha, ha, ha...! – I love it when we laugh together like two school boys.

– Lunch is served! – we hear Mary's voice with a foreign accent.

– Come on, Jorge. Mary made a chicken curry with curry that's already making my mouth water. You'll love it, I'm sure. I assume you like chicken?

– I sure do. Besides, our long walk together was very appetising.

Food for the Soul

The closer we get to the entrance of the house, the more intense a delicious scent rises into my nose. There's no question about it, Mary is a true master chef.

– Hello, Jorge. How are you? – Mary greets me and takes a pot off the stove.

– Good, Mary. Very well, thank you. It smells simply wonderful in here.

– It'll taste even better, ha, ha, ha ... – Joe's already sat down at the table and looks as if he's about to pounce on the chicken. His face is radiant like a little boy receiving an award. Sit down, Jorge!

As we all sit at the table, Joe stretches his arms out on both sides so we can grab his hands. Mary takes his right hand and I take his left. Instinctively, Mary and I also stretch our arms across the table to form a circle with our hands. Joe closes his eyes and says a table blessing.

– Infinity, thank you for the wonderful food you have brought to our table. Please, through their nutrients, give our minds and bodies the strength to make this world a better place from day to day. Furthermore, we ask you that people everywhere may enjoy food as good as we do. Thank you also for all the blessings of this day, including the friendship with our dear Jorge, with whom we would like to share this blessed meal. Thank you, Infinity – he opens his eyes and smiles at us like a child. – Let us eat now...! – Joe begins to fill our plates.

At first, we enjoy this true feast. Mary tells me how she and Joe met, he talks about the latest scientific achievements. I try to get involved in both subjects and at the same time enjoy the delicious food to the fullest.

– And your children? – I dare you to ask me a personal question.

– Unfortunately, it hasn't worked out with children – Mary informs me.

– Oh, I'm sorry, Mary. Excuse me, please.

– Don't worry about it. Mary calms me down about the clumsy way I put my foot in my mouth. – It's long over. But why don't you and Sara have kids?

– When we got married three years ago, we wanted a child or two. Since then, however, we have been economically struggling to survive. Not only is the mortgage on the house we bought a burden on us, but I also had to give up my better paid job because my former company was dissolved. Sara only works part-time at the moment... To cut to the chase, we've been putting it off for lack of money.

– What a pity, this problem comes up more often than you think – Mary reaches out her arm to me and caresses my hand tenderly. But don't worry, you're at a turning point for the better. As Joe tells me, you're working on boosting your network marketing efforts. Many who have worked seriously with Joe have managed to improve their lives. Take advantage of this opportunity, and financial shortages will soon no longer be an obstacle to your desire to have children.

– I will, Mary. Thanks for your support and for letting me have Joe for so long.

Joe looks at me with a smile and fetches a fruit platter for dessert. When he sits down again, he starts cutting up an apple.

– Here, have a piece. They're from Manuel's garden. His wife is a real master of organic farming. Remember the fisherman?

– Yes, of course I remember him. The fisherman with the smile on his face.

– It's important to take care of your health with healthy food. We've always tried to buy as natural products as possible.

– Yes, within the bounds of our possibilities, we too attach importance to good quality food. In the end, you save on medical costs. My grandmother used to say: "You are what you eat".

– Your grandmother was quite right. Healthy nutrition is also crucial to being able to master the challenges of everyday life with the appropriate strength. Actually, it's obvious, but people generally eat less and less, so it doesn't seem to be a given. It's nice that you feed your body consciously, but do you also pay attention to sufficient soul food?

– I should feed my soul? – Once again, Joe surprises me with his unusual approach. – I don't understand.

– That's right, your soul. What do you feed it?

– Like I said, I don't understand.

– Please write down the following in your notebook: "Fourth Magical Lever: Provide your soul with suitable nourishment" – I diligently note down the words without understanding what Joe means by that. – The emphasis is on "suitable" because you feed it unconsciously anyway. The problem is that you may be feeding it poor quality nutrients.

– Joe, I don't understand.

– Let me see how I can make you understand, Jorge. How many meals a day do you provide for your body? – he looks at me seriously when I ask him.

– I'm sure it's a mistake not to have snacks between meals, so basically three times, breakfast, lunch and dinner.

– Okay, three times. Then you should remember to give your soul as well as your body good food three times a day. To be honest, however, I would already be satisfied with a proper breakfast from now on.

– A breakfast for the soul? But what is my soul supposed to eat for breakfast, Joe?

– Probably your current soul breakfast consists of anxiety and haste, spiced with a pessimistic world view. or, as Mary calls it, "fake news broadcasts".

– I'm still not following you, Joe. Please try to make yourself clear.

– Well, Jorge, most people get up in the morning in a hurry. Immediately they start to have all kinds of problems in their heads, causing mental stress and anxiety. The upcoming day becomes dull in their minds. Does that sound familiar?

– Oh yes, in the morning I'm always in a hurry and my head is always buzzing. I usually get up in a pretty negative mood.

– Don't worry, you're no exception. This pessimism comes from the viruses we were talking about. This kind of food is fatal for our souls and our coming day. And probably that's why you turn on the TV with the early news, so that you don't have to listen to yourself so much. This is not only true for the morning, but also for the midday and evening news at mealtimes. Am I right?

– Yes, you are. Sara and I like to be well informed.

– I don't want to judge you or anyone else, most people watch the news for breakfast, lunch and dinner. And usually it's not good news, on the contrary, it's extremely negative pictures and news. The mass media today are characterised by an exaggerated sensationalism. Watching it, one gets the feeling that there is nothing good left in the world. It is astonishing how little positive news is reported in the media. Apparently, they think that it does not sell well and does not attract interest. Personally, I found out about unbiased and positive media and I haven't watched news broadcasts for years. I can assure you that this kind of food provides your soul with nothing but good food, which will support you to manage the challenges of the day. Imagine that you provide your body with spoiled food for breakfast. Your day will certainly not be very pleasant, and you will spend half of it in the toilet. Ha-ha-ha...!

– Agreed, but how do I feed my soul in a suitable way?

– Instead of suitable, you could call it consciously. I tell you what Mary and I have been doing for years. When I get up, I sit in bed for a few minutes and say thank you for the new day I have. As important as good food is to the soul, it is to the soul to let go of the bad. Therefore, the television is never switched on under any circumstances. Instead, we listen to happy music that provides our souls with the necessary "minerals". During breakfast, I read a book for personal development, which provides my soul with the appropriate "vitamins". Thanks to our internet expert Mary, we have recently started watching motivation videos. On the net, you can find high quality productions with wonderful messages for self-development. Remember the power of words. Finally, at bedtime, I thank the Infinity for all the good that happened to me that day. I even thank for the obviously bad things, because I know they carry the seed of goodness within them that is to come. We will deal with gratitude in more detail. For now, it is crucial that you and Sara stop serving garbage to your souls and provide them with happy and motivating food. You only need to overcome yourself and try. The results will come as quickly as they come.

– I've been thinking about the TV news a lot myself, Joe. But we get up and turn on the TV almost subconsciously.

– That is why I used the word "conscious". Our brain lets us do most things automatically. According to scientists, it consumes many resources and therefore acts unconsciously to save energy 95 % of the time. This results in the famous habits that make us their slaves for the rest of our lives. The good news is that we can change these habits. If we change our habits, we also bring about a change in our lives. Therefore, you have to be absolutely honest with yourself. But we will also come back to the habits and how to change them later in detail. For the moment, I would like you not only to believe me, but to try to do so yourself. Turn on music instead of TV, read, watch motivational videos for breakfast, and if you are ready, also at noon to get through the afternoon. If you are tired and feel like watching TV at dinner time, then you should at least choose something funny. If you do the same at bedtime and spend a few minutes to say thank you for the day you've had, you'll sleep better. In addition, you will wake up the next morning with a completely new attitude towards life. Your attitude will become noticeably more positive and things will go easier for you. Remember to reprogram your brain and learn to learn.

Joe asks Mary to select several of the videos he mentioned. Helpfully she connects the laptop and gets to work. Just a minute later she finds something suitable. Joe asks me to use the headphones so that I can get more involved in the situation. Both get up and go to the kitchen to leave me alone on the sofa. I start the video. Film scenes are accompanied by voices with motivating messages. In fact, the emotive words make me feel more and more optimistic, but at the same time I feel angry that I am no longer trying to bring about a positive change in my life. The voices of the speakers become louder as the messages become more emotional. They shake me up and finally cause a violent outburst of emotion. Tears run down my cheeks, I feel deeper and deeper inside myself, and my emotions are as intense as never before. Joe was right, now I feel ready and almost obliged to make a change in my life. The thing with the videos really works. I didn't think they would be so convincing. In the end, I take off the headphones and lean back in the sofa with my eyes closed. I take a deep breath to process the adrenaline rush.

– Well, how was it? – Joe takes a seat next to me. – The motivation is literally pouring out of your eyes. Ha-ha-ha...!

– Wow...! – I snort and try to calm my breath. I have experienced extremely intense minutes in which countless things and situations have gone through my head. All of this has totally stirred me up. It seems incredible how such a short video can trigger so many feelings. Joe, I want a real change in my life and I'm ready for anything.

– First of all, calm down, one thing at a time. For now, I want you to understand, as you have seen for yourself, that words are the gateway to feelings that carry as much or even more weight than words. Feelings move the world, and one of the most effective ways to create feelings is through words. This is true for good and for bad. Your viruses have been planted in you through words that have become attached to your hard drive as feelings. Change the words you speak, think, and hear, and your feelings will change. Change your feelings, and you will change your life. Although it is also based on logical arguments, our business is fundamentally emotional. Therefore, I advise you to become familiar with controlling your emotions. Feelings are like anchor points. That's why I advised you yesterday to sign the agreement as soon as you landed. At that moment, you were in a positive mood and felt strong. You will remember it forever and associate good feelings with it. Please answer me one question now: Do you think your morning or afternoon will go the same if you supply your brain with some videos of this kind instead of all the news garbage?

— The video triggered feelings in me that are not at all comparable with the depressive information of the news broadcasts. Something touched me so deeply in my innermost being that I felt like tackling the life I had not felt in me for a long time with exuberant energy.

— I'm glad to hear it. Your soul will be immensely grateful for such nutrients. Coupled with a stop to the intake of negative and therefore indigestible news, you will notice a radical change in your state of mind. There will always be bad moments in life and in business when you would like to throw everything away. Remember, I was about to jump off that cliff. These tools help us even at such low points. Our memory doesn't reach far, so we have to keep reminding ourselves of such messages that connect us to our true self and make us fight for our dreams. The members of your team will also support you with edifying messages. This is one of the great advantages of working in a network marketing company: You'll never be short of people to inspire and motivate you. On the other hand, you can't expect the thoughts from the videos to come from your friends or family. From the little you have told me, I conclude that they hardly speak of such things, and certainly not in these words. More likely they will confront you with conflicting messages. You should therefore make regular use of videos and books of this kind, which can often accompany you as best friends and allies. In any case, make it a rule to consciously nourish your soul several times a day. In this way your life will change, I can assure you. The decisive moments are waking up and bedtime. But as I said, I would be satisfied with a nutritious breakfast for your soul to begin with.

— All right, let me see if I can convince Sara to keep the TV off. As I mentioned, she likes to be well-informed.

— Explain what we have just discussed. If she doesn't understand and wants to keep watching TV, don't engage in any discussion. You can just have breakfast with headphones on and watch the videos on the laptop. Eventually, she'll understand. Give the people close to you time to notice changes that they don't understand at first. It's logical and shouldn't cause you any headaches. They have their own program about life in general and their image of you. Now you come up with a different way of doing things and they are not used to it. Their reaction is really a sign that you are changing and doing things in a new way. You will get different results because of this. Positive and constructive changes necessarily lead to the same kind of results. The important thing is not to deviate from your path. By the way, I didn't even ask what Sara said about your tandem jump – his look challenges me to give him an answer I don't want to give him.

– To be honest, she didn't really like it. She is a little anxious and worried that something could have happened to me. She also accused me of not flying because of my fear of heights, but that I was now doing this parachute jump. Relationship issues.

– I think she should have been happy with you for overcoming your fear of heights. As I noticed from various details, Sara has difficulties with you trying and learning new things on your own. I never felt that way with Mary, even though we lived together for almost thirty years. Over all these years we have shared many beautiful things together, but we have never stood in the way of each other's development. In this respect, we have always respected each other. I'm not asking you to end your relationship with Sara, that's not my point at all. You should only realise that Sara has things to learn about life and herself. You need a lot of patience and trust in your point of view until she is ready. Has Sara supported you in your business activities lately?

– Actually, not really. From the beginning, she thought the business was a scam and that I was being fooled. She said I was only losing my money and my time. She never came with me to the meetings either, and she's bad-mouthed it. That's why she did not agree that I come here and learn more about network marketing from you.

– More with me than from me, I'd say. First of all, I congratulate you for getting into the business despite this strong headwind and for fighting your way here. I can well understand how difficult this was for you. What Sara is not yet clear about is that as a reward for doing things you don't like for a while, you get to do what you really want for the rest of your life. Soon she will realise that you are doing it for her as well, to give her the quality of life you want. If she knew that this is the solution to realise your desire to have children and to give the child(ren) a great life, she would act and think differently. She just does not know it yet. One step at a time, my friend. By the way, I take the liberty of appearing as an alchemist again on this occasion - he looks at me mischievously at these words. - I can tell you, these problems are once again a blessing.

– You with your blessing! – my forehead spontaneously furrows.

– Ha, ha, ha ...! Remember, your personal story will take you by the hand and lead you to success. It can be compared to an archive, in which a collection of small personal and concrete stories is stored. On your way to success you will have to help many people to overcome the same fears that are torturing you now. Depending on the time and the person, you will share one or the other story of your collection with that person. In so doing, you will pass on the one that most closely corresponds to the situation in which your conversation partner is currently in. When they notice that you have experienced something similar and tell them how you have mastered it, they will have the solution and the necessary motivation in mind to continue fighting. And the good news is that what happened to you with Sara is happening to many, so you will be able to help them a lot with your personal experience. Often relationship partners are the worst enemies of our business, at least initially. As a result, more people than we like give up the business before they understand it properly. In the vast majority of cases that I know, partners change their attitude with a little patience and persuasion as soon as their lives start to improve significantly. Many of them also turn out to be great entrepreneurs in the end. Build up a lot of trust in yourself and faith in your project as well as loving patience. Do not hold it against her. Just remember that she too carries with her all her acquired fears, misconceptions and complexities. You do not have to be her judge, but her role model. Give her the attention and care she deserves, but never at the expense of your own development. In this regard, I recall the last verse of the poem by William Ernest Henley, which became famous through the film Invictus over a part of Nelson Mandela's life. If you haven't seen it yet, you should definitely catch up. The verse reads as follows:

"It matters not how strait the gate,
How charged with punishments the scroll,
I am the master of my fate:
I am the captain of my soul."

A moment of silence is created by the touching words of this so wonderful and poignant verse. If I really want to change my life, I must become the captain of my soul and take the direction I think is right. Sara loves me sincerely, I know that, but she drags these educated fears around with her, as Joe calls them. I will be patient with her, my family and all those who neither understand nor encourage me. I want to draw even more strength from her doubts in the future. I like the idea of using this energy as a lever. I will prove to Sara and everyone else that they were wrong not to trust me. For that I will do everything I can.

– I want to become the captain of my soul! – it takes me away involuntarily.

– Ha-ha-ha! I am pleased with your verve and your energy. You show me that we are pushing the right buttons for your metamorphosis, so that you can leave the nest that kept you small and insecure. Now, allow me, an old man to rest a little. In the meantime, do whatever you feel like doing. Make yourself at home, and you already know your room if you want to sleep a little. But keep an eye on the time so that you are ready later. We start again at six o'clock sharp. Ha, ha, ha ...!

– What are we going to do? I'm only asking so I can choose the right clothes.

– We're going to the basketball game.

– Basketball? Awesome! – I answer as surprised as I am amazed. – I've loved basketball since I was a child. For many years, I played on the school team, and not even that badly. I was famous for throwing three points at the last second to keep us from losing. It's weird. I just remembered the feeling when the coach put his trust in me and got me into the game in the last seconds. He expected me to play the heroic threesome that would secure us the victory.

– And did you score the most?

– Less often than I would have liked, I must admit. But the fact is, we did win a few games thanks to my "emergency throws". The coach trusted me for a reason.

– Then that's perfect. You can relive good old times.

– Yes, I'm sure I'll have some good memories. Besides, it's been a long time since I've watched a live game. I'll see you around. I'm gonna take a walk on your beautiful property.

– I think that's a great decision. Enjoy it the way we do. See you later, Jorge – Joe accompanies Mary, who is also climbing the stairs, to the bedrooms.

An Unforgettable Basket

After a relaxing walk through this veritable paradise, I decide to return to shower and get dressed in preparation for the mysterious basketball game. I also used the break to go over my notes. What excites me most is the approach of alchemy, as Joe calls it. In truth, he does not exaggerate it one bit. He twists and turns everything until something initially frightening turns into something that is like a gift from heaven. And all his approaches and examples are based on common sense.

When I am finished, and descend the stairs, I hear a lovely melody that makes the house even more inviting. Downstairs, I see Joe and Mary beautifully dressed up and dancing together, laughing.

– Ah, Jorge! You wanna dance, too? We have a few minutes before we have to leave.

– No, thanks. I don't have much of a sense of rhythm.

– Ha-ha-ha! Your lack of rhythm is like your fear of heights, it's pure fantasy. Come here and dance with Mary so I can get something out of the office in a hurry. She's an expert. Darling, please make sure Jorge gets this nonsense out of his head.

– Come here, Jorge. – With her index finger, Mary makes it clear to me that there is no escape. – Don't worry. It's child's play. Just get involved and try to let me lead you. Look, one, two, three and one, two, three...

To my surprise, after some advice from Mary and the inevitable steps on her feet, I realise that I am actually dancing! I can't stop being amazed. Until now I had thought I was not made for dancing. The most incredible thing is that I am relaxed and enjoy it. Of course, this angelic being simplifies everything many times over. We dance and dance and it feels great.

– Wow, Jorge, you dance! Ha-ha-ha...! – Joe's already back and he's breaking out his signature laugh. Did I promise you too much, Jorge? Just like your fear of heights, you're gonna have to face it. You look like a real pro! You see now that it was just a mental virus? When you overcome each small fear, you take a giant step forward in your personal development. I congratulate you from the bottom of my heart, Jorge.

– Thank you, Joe – I keep dancing as I speak.

– I'm sorry to interrupt this so intimate moment, but it's time. Jorge, don't forget to take your notebook, just in case – remind Joe.

– Thank you so much, Mary. This beautiful dance will be in my memory forever. Thank you for helping me overcome another fear. I promise to keep practicing with Sara.

– You really should. For your first time, you were doing really well. In my opinion, you have what it takes to be a good dancer.

– Let's go! – Tom is waiting for us in the car and I don't want to be late.

We get into the car and barely half an hour later we stop in a rather poor suburban quarter where I have never been before. The sports facility we head for makes an equally modest impression. Apparently, this team does not play in the first or second division. As I enter the sports field, I notice how many people greet Mary and Joe effusively. A remarkably well-dressed gentleman emerges from the crowd, approaches the couple and almost reverentially welcomes them. As he is introduced, I assume he is the president of the club. He talks to a boy who shortly afterwards brings us caps from the local team, which we immediately put on as a gesture of support.

Joe suggests Mary and I find a seat in the only available row of seats while he clarifies something with the club president. The audience is mixed, but dominated by young boys and girls, all well dressed in team shirts and caps. The overall atmosphere is very similar to my basketball matches at school. Those were magical moments back then. Piece by piece, memories of all the teammates I haven't seen for years are rising in me. In such moments, you realise how quickly life passes.

– Mary, what teams did we come here for? Judging by the basketball court, it's not exactly an elite team – I find out while wiping the seats with a handkerchief.

– No, of course it's not an elite team. It consists of young people from socially disadvantaged families. In this neighbourhood, money is not exactly on the street, and Joe has been providing economic support for years. There used to be not even a basket here. Joe has always been very generous in all kinds of initiatives to improve people's lives. As you could see, we're quite popular here.

– So, the game's about to start – Joe interrupts us, holding popcorn for everyone and sits between the two of us. – We have an important match coming up today. If we win, we'll go into the playoffs for advancement.

It's strange how much Joe is obviously excited about this game. The referee blows the whistle. The boys on the local team don't play that badly, but the opposing team has a player who is superior to the others both in size and in physical strength and quality. He also looks as if he were three or four years older. This is a big disadvantage for our team, who are four points behind in the first quarter.

– My boys are playing great, what do you think? Joe uses the break for a question. – They too had to learn a lot from scratch, like you're learning right now. They come from a very difficult environment, but they have managed to combine their potential. As they have discovered, the help of a team and the focus on a common goal enables them to achieve things they could never have dreamed of. Several of the team's boys have already been signed up and are performing in higher leagues.

– That is ingenious – again, my reaction is one of genuine amazement. Mary has already told me that you are fully committed to these young people.

– Yes, one of the things that multilevel marketing has enabled me to do is to get involved in numerous charitable projects. You could say that for health reasons, my main professional activity for years has been philanthropy. I think it's wonderful to put the money that I have left over and that they lack in the service of a good cause. That was a true serendipity.

– What does that mean? I've never heard that word before.

– You haven't? Serendipity refers to a happy and unexpected observation. For example, Alexander Fleming, when he accidentally discovered penicillin

– And what does that have to do with us?

– Well, when you get into network marketing, you are looking for a passive income that will give you the financial independence that you have been longing for. Over the years and with the rise in the business, you'll discover undreamt-of opportunities. In the beginning my focus was on money and freedom, but in the end, I support many people to improve their lives. On the one hand, in business by my example, and on the other hand, like with these young people. And you realise that the biggest gain lies in the person you have become on this path, the best version of yourself. This is an extraordinary case of serendipity, isn't it?

– It is indeed. This aspect of the business is still a little far away for me, but with your example of personality development and your wise words, everything is taking on a much clearer shape. I thank you from the bottom of my heart, Joe.

– You're welcome, Joe. For now, just concentrate on getting through a successful Step One and enjoy it to the fullest. All in good time. Now, let me ask you a question: Have you noticed the opposing team's player that stands out both in size and skill?

– Yes, I have. He also seems to be a few years older than the rest.

– What do you think would happen if he were to go up against our boys alone?

– On his own? He wouldn't stand a chance. He wouldn't even have a chance.

– That's the way you did it in your business. "Fifth Magical Lever: Make the system work for you." Using the power of the system is the biggest advantage of network marketing compared to other forms of business. And the power of teamwork is undoubtedly the core of the system. Many people have difficulties with teamwork, but large projects always require large and well-coordinated teams. In most cases, you will not get very far alone. Good coordination and the sharing of responsibilities among the team members strengthens everyone together.

– Is that why we came to the game? To prove to me how badly I worked in the team?

– No, that's what happened. You know, my life is full of coincidences. Let's get back to the subject at hand. You wanted to build the business on your own, without the power of the team. Network marketing is not a one-man game like chess, it's a team sport like basketball. And even in professional chess there is a support team behind the players. Learning teamwork is not easy, but necessary. Here you can see boys playing together who have fought each other on the street before. They had to overcome their differences in order to pull together. That wasn't easy at times, but they managed to do it. You said you didn't like some of the leaders, so you wanted to do it alone. This is a serious mistake for any kind of teamwork. Disagreements have to stay in the locker room, like with these guys, because internal conflicts do great damage to all team members. In basketball as in multilevel marketing, there is no in-between, either everybody wins or they lose.

– But I can't help it if I don't like some of them. My neighbour, for example, is starting to get on my nerves. He keeps calling me to see if I have people he can present the business to. Furthermore, I almost never see invited guests at his place. And to be honest, I'm tired of his demands.

– You don't have to like everybody, I'm not saying that. You think all the guys on the team like each other? They certainly don't. But they understand that if they want to win, they have no choice but to get along with each other. Either everybody wins or everybody loses, that's what they've learned. Network marketing is one of the forms of business that is nowadays called "win-win". To achieve good results, you have to make sure that your team is doing well, and vice versa. It becomes problematic when mental viruses attack and personal interests begin to assert themselves. People then start to see the business as a solo game, which usually means its end. Some types of entrepreneurs want more than anything else a team that is willing to provide comprehensive support. In return, beginners in this business often make the mistake of not appreciating this most important resource. They don't use it because their superiors "don't look good" to them, as they do to you. Remember that as soon as possible. Learn from the boys here. Anyway, I find what you tell me about your neighbour interesting. It seems things aren't going so well for him, huh?

– No, he's not. Several of them have already left the business in anger because of his rather bossy nature.

– This is obvious with this occurrence. In such cases, which are no exception, it is important to look further up in the hierarchy of your sponsorship structure. There you will find people with success stories who can help you much better than your neighbour. He may be your upline, but he doesn't have the personal history and experience or the success to back up his words. He clashes fully into the fatal trap number two and wants to take step two before a successful step one. Therefore, he puts pressure on you in the belief that his business depends on you. It would be more advisable for him to recruit people until a successful Step One is completed, and in the meantime to learn from those who can already look back on results. The consequences were borne by those who dropped out, and you barely escaped this fate. Such people do great harm to organisations because the real leaders hardly know about these difficulties. All you have to do at this stage, Step One, is to forgive them for their inappropriate actions and look further up the sponsorship structure of your team for people who are suitable to help you achieve your goals. What distinguishes a true leader from an upline whose only success is to have entered the business before you and to have recommended it to you is demonstrated results and a history of self-development. Memorise the feeling you feel in the relationship with your neighbour so that you do not make the same mistake with others in the future. The secret is to make an effort so that your results speak for themselves. The time to hold workshops and get applause will come for you in

Step Two. Until then, rely on the power of the team wherever possible. And instead of thinking that you don't like them, focus on their merits, of which they certainly have more to offer than their bad points. Put aside your prejudices and their good qualities will reveal themselves to you as if by magic. Your role in the team will change as you move up in the business, and so will your story. If you do not use this lever properly, you will make money for a while, but never achieve financial independence. Approach your uplines and mentors from within. Do not wait for them to contact you. Show them your interest and willingness to work hard, and you will undoubtedly find open doors.

– So far, I haven't had much to do with them, but you can count on me to intensify my search for contact with them from now on. As for my neighbour, I think I'll tell him to go to hell the next time he comes in with his demands.

– Take it easy. As I said, try to excuse his behaviour. It's his mental viruses that are causing him to behave this way. Set a good example, so he can understand and deal with it in a new way. Remember, life is like a big mirror that reflects everything we send out. The seventh point of the agreement will help you do that.

– The seventh point? What is it again? – A felt eternity passes, in which Joe looks at me and waits until my memory starts. The infinite patience! Forgive me for forgetting that so quickly.

– It's all right. You're just beginning to understand the concept.

– Thank you for your patience with me, Joe.

– It's a real pleasure. There's one more thing I'd like to say.

– Go ahead, Joe – I ask him, with the pen in my hand.

– It does you good to confide in leaders and people with results. Remember our conversation about mirror neurons? Let me remind you again that because of these neurons we unconsciously imitate the people we are with. In contrast to other forms of business or employment, multilevel marketing allows you to get in touch with entrepreneurial, combative and often successful people. In daily life, this is not so easy. If you only deal with "commentators", you will end up commenting just like them. In contrast, you will achieve great things if you surround yourself with "doers". With the right attitude and excellent work, your uplines will be happy to share their experience and friendship with you. Pay careful attention to their actions. Their great success means that they have done many things right, that is, they are real "doers". Your business does not depend on them, but with them at your side it will be much easier for you. If you recommend the business to someone, remember that you are also offering them the opportunity to meet such positive role models.

The basketball game is now at another pause. I write down the details of all these considerations in my notebook so I don't forget anything. Looking at the scoreboard, I realise that we are eight points behind. It's getting harder and harder to catch up. A melody comes out of the loudspeakers, and the gentleman Joe introduced to me at the beginning of the game stands in the middle of the court and speaks into the microphone.

– Good afternoon to you all and thank you for coming to cheer the boys on so valiantly in this decisive match for advancement. As usual, someone from the audience will now throw the "super basket". Today, however, it does not run as usual, there is a short-term change. This time the successful pitcher will not be happy about a dinner for two, but will not win anything.

– Ohhhhhh! – Disappointment about the changed rules is spreading in the audience.

– Please calm down...! – the President continues – in return, our esteemed sponsor, Mr Goodman, will donate a minibus to the club for the team rides when the ball lands in the basket.

– Ole, ole, ole... – the mood in the audience is rising again and I am still busy with my notes.

– Instead of drawing lots for a pitcher, Mr Goodman has asked me to let someone specific throw. Apparently, he was a great player in his youth and has a good chance to make this donation possible. His name is Jorge Guzmán. Applause please for Jorge!

Did I hear my name or am I not quite right my mind? I look up at Joe from the notebook so he can give me an answer.

– Come on, Jorge, you gotta throw! – Joe calmly tells me.

– What do I have to do? – I feel like saying a rude word, but I'm too scared to even speak. – Why are you doing this to me, Joe? What am I going to do now?

– It's very simple. All you have to do is throw from the centre of the court. Don't get upset. Just enjoy the moment. Remember when you were a basketball player. I know you can do it because I believe in you. Think of the guys riding on their own bus and concentrate. Don't believe your brain, but listen to your heart. Relax and shoot.

– I also know you can do this, Jorge – Mary says, encouragingly.

– What a responsibility, Joe. How can you do it, Joe? – I turn my eyes away from Joe, turn around and walk towards the centre of the court where the president is waiting for me with the ball in my hand.

– I can do it! Take it easy! – I try to give myself courage. I reach the middle of the court, where the President hands me the ball after introducing me and informing me that I have two attempts. All at once, apart from a few individual shouts of encouragement, there is silence in the seats. I look briefly at the ball, take a deep breath and try to remember my throwing style. To take the pressure off, I want to make sure that a miss is not too bad. However, a hit and the bus for the boys would be great. All right, let's do it! I take a challenging look at the basket, dribble a couple of times, take another look at it and make the appropriate calculations in my head. Then I align myself in the centre of the court and throw with the momentum I think is necessary without letting the basket out of my sight. The ball flies towards the basket, the direction seems to be right. Let's see if it goes in. From this distance, it may not even touch the ring. These short moments stretch out noticeably. I see the ball touching the back of the ring, but not falling in. It rebounds away upwards.

– Oh no, it misses. That was to be expected. Too bad, I was close. I got one more shot, right? – I ask the president, who is still standing next to me.

– Wait, wait...! – he says and keeps his eyes on the basket.

I also look at the basket and am amazed to see that the ball falls once more onto the outermost part of the ring, which slows down its swing. It then hits the board and begins to circle the ring like a juggling demonstration. The ball spins one round, then two, and at the third it seems to fall out for good. But then it makes a strange spin around itself and to my amazement it seems to land in the net. I can hear everyone in the audience screaming at the same time. They rise from their seats and throw caps and scarves into the air.

– Was it in? – I still ask the President in disbelief.

– Of course, you did it – he replies and almost knocks me down with a strong hug.

– Jooorgeeee, Jooorgeeee...! – I hear the audience in the row of seats shouting my name in chorus as they clap their hands tirelessly.

I look over at Mary and Joe. They look over at me joyfully and lift their thumbs up to congratulate me from afar. I too raise my thumbs up. I still can't believe it, it's maddening.

After congratulations from different sides and another hug from the president, I go back to the bank. Everyone congratulates me and wants to shake my hand. It almost becomes too much for me. Now I know how a rock star feels with his fans. Arriving at our seats, my two friends are already holding out their arms, and the three of us merge into a hug. For a few unforgettable seconds, we remain like this. I will never forget this moment.

I still can't believe it! – I say without letting go of her.

– I've told you, you can do this. – whispers Joe in my ear – Believe more in yourself, you're a real whiz.

I can't stop thinking about my basket, especially on my first try. Besides, I can't get the words "I believe in you", which Joe gave me on the way before throwing it, out of my mind. Frankly, I'm not used to having them said in my life. Joe has already talked about the power of words, but can they really do so much to make a throw a hit?

– You have made me poor, Jorge, ha, ha, ha ... I'm kidding. You should be proud of yourself. Thanks to your great performance, you've made the boys overjoyed.

– Thanks, Joe. One thing I can't get out of my mind. Do you think the words of trust you spoke to me before you threw me the ball had anything to do with my score?

– Absolutely. We've already discussed the power of words. They release really powerful creative energy. This applies not only to the words spoken, but also, as I said, to the words thought and the attitude towards something or someone. I didn't just say empty words, I really felt them inside me. I fully believe in you. What is missing in this equation is that you believe in yourself again. Remember the fourth point of your agreement?

– Let me see...! "To have complete trust in my abilities and those of others" – this time my answer comes much more fluently than before.

– Right, full trust in yourself and in others! That's why I pointed out to you how important it is to focus on the strengths of your team members, both uplines and downlines. If you really trust in their possibilities and abilities, they will show them. We create the world as we experience it with our attitudes. The difficult part is that our attitudes are contaminated with the psychological viruses mentioned above. As a result, our reality often does not look the way we would like it to, unless we change our attitude towards the world, life and people. Have confidence in all their possibilities. If your downlines are not doing anything, do not lose faith in them. Just be patient and make your contribution by being an example for them day by day. Everyone follows his own rhythm of development. I have met people who took months or even years to understand all these things, but in the end, they succeeded, sometimes quite considerably. Respect their rhythm of development, it makes things much easier. You need to have faith in them, but as far as I can tell, the first thing you need to do is have more faith in yourself. What do you think, Jorge, why would anyone believe in you if you don't? Once again, we're talking about common sense, aren't we?

– All right, Joe, but it's not that simple.

– And what would be easier? Not to believe in you?

– Oh, boy, when you put it that way...

– It doesn't make a lot of sense. Life is a lot harder when you don't believe in yourself. So, what is easy and what is difficult? It's all relative.

– You're right, I've gotta start building more confidence in myself. I promise you, I'll make an effort to have more faith in my abilities. Actually, I've always felt that I have untapped potential. I think now is the time to prove it.

– Absolutely. And, from what I can tell, you should have more faith in your business. Otherwise, it's going to be a lot harder for you to recommend it with complete confidence. Let's deal with this later. Now let's see if the boys can still raise their score in this very important game.

– All right, Joe.

The game is pretty even in the third quarter, although our team will lose by eleven points at the end. Meanwhile, the mood in the crowd is depressed because of the unfortunate result. In the short break before the last quarter Joe gets up from his seat without a word and goes to the bench of the home team. He speaks to them as if he were their coach. After a conversation of just over a minute and the typical "battle roar", he shakes the coach's hand and returns to us.

I prefer not to ask and to pretend I didn't notice. The boys go into the last quarter with a better performance. Thanks to some fast baskets, which reduce the gap to seven points, the crowd gets back in the mood. Point by point they fight back until only two points are needed in the last minute. The entire audience cheers on the players incessantly. I would never have thought that a match with youngsters could be so exciting. At the very last moment, one of our team throws a basket off the three-point line, putting us one point ahead. All together the spectators jump from their seats and rage even louder. The guest team throws from a distance, but due to time pressure and the opposition of the home team, they don't even hit the ring. With the final whistle, everyone storms onto the court as if on command. They put the boy with the victorious three-point throw on their shoulders, but in truth the congratulations and hugs are for the whole team. A true ecstasy of joy spreads around the court and we too run forward to wish the boys all the best. The congratulations addressed to me also remind me again of my successful basket, which still seems like a dream. Hugs and laughter characterise this game. All's well that ends well. Then I notice Joe walking over to the players of the losing team, who are sitting with their heads hanging down at the other end of the field. Joe sits down with them for a few minutes, after which they say goodbye to him with a handshake and much happier faces. When we have found each other again and said goodbye to everyone, we make our way out of the sports facility between the helpers.

– Let me ask you something, Joe. What did you say to our boys to help them make this fabulous recovery?

– Basically, just that I believe in their abilities as much as you do.

– Wow, once again, causality.

– As you can see, life is very strange and there are lots of causalities once you pay attention to them.

– I noticed that.

We climb into the car and obviously drive back to the country house. Up to now I have never seen Joe with a mobile phone, but now he pulls one out and seems to be writing a message to someone.

– Unbelievable, Joe, what has happened in this game. With a few simple words miracles have happened. I don't know, sometimes I think you are a magician or something like that.

– Those weren't just words, they were sincere feelings that I conveyed to you through words. Earlier I believed in you and that still holds true. And no, I am not a magician at all. As you know, I prefer to think of myself as an alchemist. Have you forgotten alchemy again?

– No, of course I remember. But the thing with my basket today was not only alchemy, it seemed to me the work of a true magician.

– Ha, ha, ha...! – this time Mary also joins in the laughter. Alchemy and magic are similar in some aspects, especially in words. We could say I am a word magician, like Mary, Tom, you and all the people in the world. We all create magic with our words. The important question is only whether you use white or black magic, depending on the type of words you choose. Speaking of black magic, please take your notebook and write down what you have written, because I am now delivering the "Third Fatal Trap: Gossip".

– Gossip?

– I think I have to take you to the doctor to see if you have wax in your ears. Ha-ha-ha...! Look, Jorge, gossip could be considered the opposite of edification. Over the many years of my multilevel marketing experience, I have seen some teams go under because they used the words to spread gossip about the other team members. Many people seem to suffer from this mental illness. I call it illness because it is comparable to blindness. These people clearly see the splinter in the other person's eye, but not the plank in their own. They also do not see the harm they do to others. Nor do they understand that this action is against their own interests. They see nothing, are blind and behave like black magicians who invent or exaggerate malicious rumours. They are usually frustrated people who fall into the trap of envy, which is another virus. As I said, they do considerable damage to everyone, including themselves. We are in the same boat. If you speak ill of your parent company, you are referring to your project. If you take it out on your team, it will affect your business. Gossip is nothing but black magic. Avoid speaking ill of others, especially since rumours are highly contagious. Always stay away from those who use them, because they overshadow your present and your future. "Doers" are not in the habit of gossiping. They are too busy making their dreams come true and have no time for foolishness. Usually, "commentators" are professional gossips. Their views usually don't build anyone up, but criticise them without understanding. They understand everything too quickly to have understood nothing in the end. Never fall into this trap, Jorge. You better edify with positive words and focus your attention on your partners' good sides. This will make you grow in wisdom and wealth, and you will also have so much more fun in your business. When you meet such a person, forgive him and respect his rhythm, but do not fall into his trap. Although your business doesn't depend on them, you should be careful to recognise such people and politely put them in their place so that they stop gossiping. Sometimes it will work, other times it won't, but don't let yourself be distracted from your path. Most of the time, they go off on their own when they find that their shabby practices have ruined their own business. That's how it will end, their organisation will go down the drain. Live gossip, and your business will go under. Be a model of true integrity, and your business will flourish despite the existence of such people.

Back at the cottage Mary goes ahead and opens the door.

– Mary, darling, we'll be right behind you. I want to talk to Jorge about a few things before dinner.

Mary turns around and gives us her blessing with a twinkle in her eye. Judging by the direction we go back to the garage.

– Are you able to cycle, Jorge?
– I haven't ridden a bike in a long time, but I'm good at it.
– Brilliant. Let's take a little ride. You can take Mary's bike.

After we adjust the seat height, we get on the mountain bikes and choose one of the country tracks. During the ride, the beauty of the surroundings once again takes over completely. The colours of the countless plants in contrast to the different shades of green and in combination with the soft light of this spring evening add up to a landscape that gives me a pleasant peaceful feeling.

– Yesterday we talked about eagles. Have you ever seen one up close? – Joe asks me, without taking his eyes off the trail.

– Honestly, no.

– Well, in a few minutes you're going to be facing a wonderful golden eagle up close. It's a wonderful animal, you'll love it.

We keep on biking until we come to a nice wooden house behind a hill. In front of it stands a gentleman with a bundle in his arms. As we get closer, I recognise Manuel the fisherman. And up close, the bundle turns into a big bird. That must be the eagle Joe was talking about.

– Good evening, Manuel – we greet him one by one.

– Good evening, Joe? How's it going, Jorge?

– Very well, Manuel, thank you – I return the compliment and can't take my eyes off the eagle.

Manuel gives us his left hand, because on his right arm is the giant eagle with shiny brown plumage. On his head sits a kind of leather helmet, but it does not hide his strong beak. It protrudes in front and is curved downwards as if it were a big tooth. On his mighty claws, you can see twisted dark nails with which he holds on to Manuel's arm in a protective glove. The eagle is as beautiful as it is powerful.

– What do you think of him, Jorge? – Joe looks at me, delicately stroking the plumage of the animal. Manuel is not only a great fisherman, but also an expert falconer. I still don't understand how he gets on so well with this wonder of nature – Manuel smiles proudly at his eagle. Manuel, please ask this splendour to do what I asked you to do in my message.

– All right. Keep a little distance, please, or he might hurt you with his wings.

After we have stepped back a couple of feet, Manuel takes the leather helmet off the bird of prey's head. Now you can see his sharp eyes, which leaves me speechless. After the animal has looked around and has also set its sights on us, it turns its eyes again directly on Manuel, who whistles a bit strangely. The eagle looks at him attentively as if he understands what Manuel is saying to him. A touching moment arises, and with a movement of Manuel's arm the eagle finally spreads its big wings and beats with them until it takes off.

– Wow! Spectacular! – I can't stop being amazed.

– Moreover, he will teach you part of the following lesson.

– Who him? The eagle? – I ask, and I can't take my eyes off the bird of prey.

– Ha, ha, ha ... – this time both Joe and Manuel are laughing. As I told you, nature is a great teacher. Now watch his flight very carefully.

– All right.

The eagle's flight is majestic. The predator bird no longer moves its wings as it glides over us. It does much smaller circles. Because it no longer flaps its wings, I assume that it will return to Manuel's arm, but the eagle seems to be continuing its ascent. I see him getting smaller and smaller, but his wings don't move, not a single flap of his wings for several minutes. At the same time, it is rising higher and higher in an upward spiral until only a small dot in the sky is visible. Suddenly Manuel's loud whistle sounds, and the eagle grows bigger again, which is why I assume it is really coming back to us now. His descent seems to be much faster than the ascent. After a few seconds the animal sits on Manuel's arm again after a perfect landing, who shoves a delicacy into his beak as a reward.

– Come closer, Jorge, and admire him without the cap – Manuel asks me, smiling.

– It is an amazing animal with a fascinating look. And its beak represents a technical feat of nature. Manuel, the descent was incredibly fast. Out of pure curiosity I would like to know at what speed he was travelling – my comments probably expose me as an ignoramus in this area.

– When the golden eagle is relaxed on the road as it was at the beginning, it reaches about 50 km/h, when it nosedives at the end it can have reached about 240 km/h.

– 240 kilometres per hour? My goodness, that's why he came back so quickly. Thank you, Manuel, for the time with your eagle. I shall never forget it.

– You're welcome, Jorge, it was a pleasure. We can do it again sometime.

– Yes, but not today – Joe's getting back on his bike and asking me to do the same. – Now we must go, Mary's waiting for us with dinner.

We say goodbye to Manuel and go back the same way we came. Already on the estate we get off and sit down on a wooden bench next to a beautiful oak tree.

– What do you think the teachings of the eagle might consist of?

– I don't know exactly what you mean, Joe – he's always with his riddles. – Perhaps you're referring to the fact that it took him longer to climb than to dive.

– In this case I mean something else, but that thought also seems very interesting to me. The lesson I have been talking about is that the eagle has shown you the same thing that you offer to all the people you want to introduce network marketing to.

– Please explain this to me, Joe.

– As you may have noticed, the eagle never flapped its wings once in its ascent.

– Yes, it's incredible how he almost vanished from view without a flap of his wings. He went into a kind of upward spiral.

– Exactly! Birds of prey are professionals at detecting warm air flow that allow them to ascend without effort. Such a warm air flow or upwind helps them to achieve more power with the same or even less effort, as we have just seen.

– Great, but what does this have to do with my offer?

– Well, you also offer an upward spiral, ha, ha, ha ...! – he bends over when he laughs.

– What are you talking about?

— Look, Jorge, network marketing provides you with a system that works like a warm airflow, helping you to achieve results that would be unattainable under other circumstances. I'm not just talking about money, I'm talking about quality time for your family and personal and professional self-realisation. Earlier I advised you to believe more in your business. Let's take a look at the advantages of such a system compared to a job or a traditional business. You will gain more confidence in the business once you understand its power from the bottom up. These benefits will make a big difference when you offer it, build it up, and above all, enjoy it. I refer to them as the "super benefits of network marketing".

— So, get on with it, Joe.

— One of the biggest advantages of network marketing for me is that you can start doing it in your spare time. This is ingenious and would hardly be possible when building a conventional company without giving up work. Not to mention the money needed for it. And there we are at the next super advantage: You can start this business with very little money, unlike traditional business forms. I even know some people who paid the entrance fees with a credit card. Within a short time, they had paid their debt and earned money. They didn't have to contribute anything from their pockets thanks to another great advantage, namely that they earned income quickly. With other forms of business, it can take years to generate net income. At my age and with my successes, it seems ridiculous to me every time someone complains about the entrance fees for our businesses, which have totalled $180,000 million worldwide by 2015. In a normal business, you invest and risk much higher sums to get started, and later you regularly have to pay local rents, credit rates, employee salaries, insurance, vehicles or suppliers on time. But worst of all, you are left alone with the risk and cannot trust anyone else with your real situation. Here we are at the next super advantage. We've already mentioned it, namely that you can count on a team and a great company to build the business. They support, guide and complement you. The company takes care of the production of quality products, you usually don't have to worry about the monthly orders, shipping and even billing is taken care of. In addition, the leaders in the team introduce the business to your contacts in a professional manner and take over their support and training until you are ready to take over this task in an appropriate way yourself. To get into the business, all you really have to do at the beginning is to motivate people to attend the presentations, which you don't even have to give yourself. Your only task is to do something that we all do all the time without pay, namely to recommend something to someone that can improve their life. Don't you think it's great to get paid for it?

– Yes, actually, although I never really cared about money.

– I'm not in the habit of talking about money, but rather about freedom. Money is a consequence and a means to greater things. With money, you can do the greatest things you can imagine. My feeling for helping these guys is priceless. To see their happy faces today when you threw the basket was a true balm for my soul. Money is a tool that, when used well, helps you to help others. And only by helping others can you achieve true happiness. They say that he who does not live to serve, does not serve life. And therein lies another super advantage, namely that such forms of business usually work with different organisations. From day one, you will feel that your efforts are good for something other than just making money. Then, of course, there are actions that you want to take on your own or with your team. Together you are strong, and together you can do charitable work and achieve things that would never be possible on your own. I have often heard Don José say: "Everything you don't give, you lose".

– You said that very nicely, Joe. And, of course, my desire is to succeed and help others as you do. That's probably the greatest feeling of all. But with debts weighing on you and more bills than income, it doesn't look easy. All day long it's all about where you can cut expenses to pay more bills. How would you feel if you didn't even have enough to give your wife a nice birthday present?

– Do you realise that the people who spend the most time per day thinking about money are just like you with little income? It sounds paradoxical, but money gives you the opportunity not to think about money. The further you climb the upward spiral of business, the clearer it becomes that the true prize is the chance for freedom. No employment or traditional business gives you the opportunity to achieve financial independence. Although I have not been actively working for years due to health reasons, I not only receive my income monthly, but it actually increases from year to year. This is another great advantage, because if you build up the business well, your physical presence becomes unnecessary. Right now, as we sit on this beautiful bench in the middle of nature, thousands of people from my team are working on their business and supporting each other with consequent benefits for me. Even after so many years, I still marvel at the power of this business system. If I had been employed, at best I could have a modest pension to be able to make a living in my senior years. If I had been a traditional entrepreneur, I would probably have had to save all my life. A passive income of this kind is the real key to freedom.

– Thank you for bringing all these concepts to my attention in this way. I can literally feel an alchemical reaction inside me.

– Ha-ha-ha! The alchemy is remarkable. I'm glad that you understand everything and that you understand yourself in a new way. That's what I'm trying to do. Gold is usually hidden under a thin layer of lead, my friend. It's up to us to understand that and put it into practice. But let's get to one last super-advantage you only find in network marketing before we go out to dinner. You can get partners almost anywhere in the world and keep growing. Ha, ha, ha ...!

– That may be, but I don't know anybody abroad, Joe.

– Ha-ha-ha! There's no need for that. Others will see to that. The system is so powerful. You don't know anybody yet. You'd be surprised how these businesses, if done right, will spread to other countries. What's more, you have a super-efficient tool that I could not use in my time: the Internet. I must admit I missed the digital revolution, but Mary, with her boundless patience, showed me how to do video conferencing. You grew up with it and you'll find many more uses for it, but just the ability to video conference with the whole world at any time seems impressive. It's almost as if you were there in person. For business structures that start out in places without a solid team, this possibility represents a more than useful, almost unavoidable resource. Videoconferencing fits this business like a glove, not only for remote business structures under construction, but also for your national and international expansion. In no time at all you will be travelling to other cities and countries. For me, it was always a great experience to come to a completely new country and meet a multitude of friends and partners who welcomed me with open arms and offered me their help in all matters. I think after going through all these super benefits, you are starting to believe a little bit more in the business you are offering, right?

— Absolutely, Joe. What means a little, much more!

— But finding your upward spiral with all the mentioned super advantages can only support you on your way, but you have to follow it yourself. Please get on the bike.

I obey and look at him questioningly for further instructions.

— The bicycle, a lever or a warm airflow are systems that help us multiply our power. The bicycle gives you the ability to go almost anywhere, right?

— With the right level of fitness, probably so.

— However, the bicycle is a system that can multiply power but cannot generate it. How far do you think you would get without pedalling?

— Nowhere, of course.

— Nowhere, exactly. The system and the team can help you in many ways, but not pedal for you. You have to make an effort for yourself, no one can do it for you. The only thing they can help you with is multiplying your effort. But no matter with which number you multiply zero, it always comes out zero. Work for the system, and the system will work for you by multiplying your stake. Focus on offering the business to as many people as possible. Get as many rejections as you can handle. You'll have to go through this part alone. You will need to develop self-discipline because no one on the team will check your hours or the people you recruit. Not having a boss should be a blessing, but it often turns into the opposite because you are too indulgent with yourself when it comes to work. It means doing what needs to be done, not what you want to do. What usually makes all entrepreneurs achieve results is the effort to do the most unpleasant things well, because what we like comes easily anyway. You could say that successful people have simply done things that others were not prepared to do. Many fool themselves and say that business is difficult, they don't know people anymore, something is wrong with the products, etc. All just to avoid doing what they claim they want to do. They make up a thousand excuses to look good. But don't worry, if you stick to the points of the signed agreement, you won't have this problem, because the relentless honesty that comes with it cures the disease of "excuses" in no time.

– Yes, we have already discussed this disease.

– Excuse me for always coming back to some aspects, this is necessary. To understand things from the bottom up, you have to look at them from different angles. I hope it's not too much repetition.

– No problem, Joe, don't worry. I really like the way you explain things to me. You're the teacher. Besides, I never get bored studying with you. Oh, no. – I'm being ironic.

– Ha-ha-ha! – This time we can laugh together.

– It's dinner time! – After looking at the clock, Joe jumps off the bench and gets on his mountain bike – Come on, Mary will probably serve dinner right away!

The Thinking Corner

After a simple, but delicious dinner with prior thanksgiving and clearing the table together, Joe sends me a very penetrating look and directs me by hand to the hallway next to the staircase.

– You are accepted into the exclusive circle of the few people who get to know our thinking corner – with his hand still raised, he does not let me out of his sight. – Are you coming or are you staying?

– Yes, of course. I'm coming! I'd like to see this corner.

The three of us walk down the corridor and stop in the middle. Joe looks at me with a smile, then grabs a coat hook on the wall. To my surprise, he pushes it down, opening a door completely camouflaged with decoration, just like in spy movies. We step through this door and descend a staircase illuminated only by a small side light into a dark cellar. Joe goes ahead and stands by a switch.

– Welcome to our thinking corner, Jorge!

When Joe turns on the light, my mouth is open once again. A

large room lined with wood and books appears before my eyes. There must be hundreds, if not thousands, of books on the shelves along the walls. In addition, there is a wonderful pool billiard table, a reading corner with two Chesterfield sofas, a dartboard and in the corner under the stairs even a simple carved bar with a small vinotheque. The window hatches at the top of the walls are closed with small wooden shutters. It is a library as if from a dream.

– Joe, this place is amazing. I love the way you've combined books and reading with games. The library is magical.

– Ha-ha-ha! Magic library? – Joe and Mary exchange glances and nod their approval – I like the way you label things. You have a great talent for inventing fancy names.

– Well, I've always liked to read, and I like to write too. I've even written a few short stories. Sara always says I should send them to a publishing house to get them published.

– Look at this, another wonderful causality! – Joe smiles as if my statement about writing amused him.

– Which one, Joe?

– All in good time. How are you in playing billiards, Jorge? – I find it a little annoying when Joe skips my questions.

– It's been ages since I played, but after my basket this afternoon, I'm bursting with confidence, so I'm not gonna let you win without a fight.

– Ha-ha-ha! – all three of us laughing like children.

– Then let's go! – Joe challenges me and racks the balls in the starting position.

After the game, which I clearly lose, even though I did quite well, we take a seat on the original Chesterfield sofas at Mary's, who had been reading in the meantime.

– Joe, may I ask if you always say a blessing at table?

– Table blessing? We call it "Thanksgiving for the food." Yes, since I met Don José, it's become a fixture. From your question, I deduce that you don't do it regularly.

– No, in the rush we don't even think about it.

– Then we will have to discuss this subject in detail before going to bed. Did you bring your notebook downstairs?

– No, it's upstairs. I'll go and get it – I'm getting ready to get up and go up the stairs.

– Wait, no need. Sit down again, I just remembered something – he takes a book from one of the shelves while I sit down again.

– This is a present for you.

– For me? – He puts the book in my lap. It's quite big, but not very thick. I let my fingers slide over the soft leather cover, which has no indication of what's inside. I open it in anticipation of a famous work, but as befits Joe's constant surprises, all the pages are completely white.

– It's empty, Joe!

– Tell me about it! You're very observant. Ha-ha-ha!

– Come on, seriously, Joe. You want me to write notes in this precious piece of paper?

– No, of course not. For your notes, I have another – he hands me an ordinary notebook from a drawer in the table in front of us.

– Then why are you giving me this blank book?

– You told me you like to write. Keep it for a special moment when you write your first bestseller. You may not have enough time or ideas now, but that will come. In the meantime, keep it safe.

– All right, Joe. Thank you. It's a wonderful gift. I give you my word that one day all these pages will be scribbled with some great story.

– Remember the first point of the agreement when you give your word. But let's get to the point. You asked me for my thanks for the dinner. Now, listen carefully.

– I'm ready, Joe. Go ahead.

– "Magic Lever Number Six: Thanks, Thanks, and Thanks."

– A bit much thank you in the title, isn't it? – I notice.

– Ha-ha-ha! – I must have said something wrong, because the otherwise so considerate Mary is also laughing. The day you put your prejudices behind you, you will make a leap forward in your personal development. The three words have three different meanings.

– But they're the same words, Joe. Then how can they be different?

– They are three different ways of showing gratitude – this time Mary's gentle voice sets things straight.

– No one could explain better than Mary what Don José taught me about gratitude. I'm going to open a bottle of wine. Today is Saturday, and I think we've done well this week, what do you think? Ha-ha-ha! – Joe goes to the bar and with a wave of his arm, asks Mary to take over for him.

– Thank you, Joe – Mary turns to me, puts the book she was reading on the table, and looks me in the eyes. – You know, Jorge, Don José attached great importance to this subject, so he also taught me the power of gratitude and how to use it. If you learn to use it, your life will improve in every possible way.

– But why three times, Mary?

– The first thanks goes to your past. I suppose you've already talked about reconciling with the past.

– Yes, we have.

– Well, the next step is to thank for all the good and obviously bad things that have happened to you in your life in the past.

– Thanking for the bad could be more difficult – I reply.

– Are you comfortable with us? Are you enjoying this moment?

– Yeah, sure, Mary. I'm very happy to be here with you. I am honestly getting really fond of both of you and I am very grateful for your advice and your friendship.

– We love you too, Jorge. But let us go on. Do you have any pain or sickness?

– No, Mary, I'm not in pain and I'm not ill. Why?

– Then you must thank your past out of pure common sense. Any small detail in your life which would have been different could have caused you to be dead now, could have made you ill, could have caused you to suffer a serious accident with permanent disability, or could have prevented us from coming together to enjoy these days together. Everything could have been completely different if one tiny little thing in your life had looked different. I was told that in the accident with Joe, you escaped death by a thousandth of a second.

After that remark that literally pressed me into the Chesterfield sofa, she takes a sip. A strange feeling comes over my whole body. I've tried not to look at the accident from that angle, but she's right. In fact, I barely escaped death and I should consider myself lucky. I straighten up again and try to regain my composure with a deep breath.

– You're right, Mary, I have miraculously survived. From now on I could have two birthdays a year instead of one.

– Exactly, and what could have ended up as a fatal accident became a soul connection due to thousandths of a second. It's strange, but with time you realise that superficially negative events always carry a hidden gift within them. In these moments, we are asked to make an effort to rise above ourselves and to show more patience and creativity. They are true teachers in the art of living. How can one not be grateful? It would not be fair. The beautiful moments are there to savour and thank for them, the bad ones are there to learn and to be grateful. With this perspective, you can reconcile with your past, including all the people you have met in your life. Thus, gratitude helps us to forgive, and that is what distinguishes the human. Little by little you will reconcile with everything and everyone, making many things much easier for you. Gratitude changes the world from the bottom up.

– Once again lead becomes gold. Well, you're an alchemist too. Looks like you got a good teacher.

– Ha-ha ha! – Joe's laughter comes up behind me.

– As you say, it's pure alchemy – Mary continues in her tender voice. Indeed, gratitude is the strongest alchemical formula there is. But let us go on. The second form of gratitude is for the moment. As Joe used to say in one of his puns, "Rich is not who has more, but who shows more gratitude for what he has". This is really true. If you are not grateful for something, it is as if you did not have it and do not give it. I am not only referring to material things, but also to such crucial things as the affection of your loved ones or health. Strangely enough, people only think about their health when they are ill. Otherwise they forget about the hundred trillion cells that are constantly at work in our bodies so that we can speak, hear, think, see, not to forget to be able to love or to thank. As long as they are in the best of health, they take this fact for granted, do not appreciate it and are therefore not grateful for it. To take something for granted is the opposite of being grateful. Don José used to say: "Health is not everything, but without health everything is nothing". Likewise, a full table and a well-filled refrigerator are taken for granted and one is no longer grateful for them. But one forgets that millions of households in the world do not even have a fridge and hardly any food. When you suffer from a temporary illness, you become grateful for everything that is still working well in your body and draw a significant lesson. Disease can become an excellent teacher. Being grateful through and through for the moment means truly appreciating and enjoying life. This includes gratitude for the air you breathe, the light and warmth of the sun, the smile of a child, the flight of a butterfly, or the goodbye kiss of Sara when you leave the house. I can assure you, none of this lasts for eternity. But don't forget to be grateful for what you don't understand and what you don't like, because you should learn something from it, even if the lesson is still hidden from you at that moment. Practice this kind of gratitude and check its effect. Then you can decide whether you want to continue as before or continue to thank for everything. Forgiveness makes us human, gratitude in turn transforms us into wise men. Always show gratitude for everything, and you will see how life opens up for you. Answer me honestly one question: If you gave many gifts to a friend, but he was not grateful, would you continue to give him gifts?

– Well, I think I'd have had enough at some point.

– The Infinity, as we like to call the intelligence that governs the universe, has the same fate, at some point it is enough to give gifts that do not meet with gratitude. Be grateful for the gifts that life gives you day after day, and you will receive more and more of them. Believe me, the desire of the Infinity is to give you everything you desire, but first you must be grateful for those gifts you have already received. Do not take things for granted. Some people have a lot of money and are very unhappy. There are rich people who commit suicide because with all that money they have forgotten to thank for what they have and are. It happens that because of an unimportant problem at home, we lose sight of the countless gifts with which life blesses us daily.

– I completely agree with you, Mary, but when the bills flutter into the house and you have no money to pay for them, it becomes difficult to express gratitude. It's at times like this that I get frustrated and powerless. I feel like a failure and a...

– And therein lies the worst mistake you can make! – Joe suddenly interrupts me in a decisive voice. Please write in your notebook, because this is the "Fourth Fatal Trap, Self-pity". This is meant seriously, because "fatal" is to be understood here in the truest sense of the word. It is one of the most dangerous mental viruses. Self-pity is an insult to yourself and to life itself. This attitude is characteristic of cowards and can only be brought to bear in the absence of gratitude. All by itself, self-pity can activate all psychological viruses at the same time and plunge you into the deepest depression you can imagine, or even kill you. Remember, it took me by the hand to that cliff to put an end to my life after it convinced me of its self-destructive attitudes. Imagine what I would have missed. I was incredibly lucky that day. But more people than you think live in their world of self-pity without realising it. That's why I hope that the next time you are attacked by the self-pity virus, you will be thankful for everything you have, because that's exactly what the second point of your agreement says. Apply the alchemy instead of feeling sorry for yourself and see what you can learn from it. I assure you, there is always a lesson waiting for you, however small it may be. If you don't find one, just wait and see. It will appear on its own. Often you will find it after hours or even minutes. In other cases, it may take years or even decades before your mind is completely clear. Patience will then be your best ally. One thing is certain, however, that sooner or later a benefit or lesson will reveal itself. Patience is another part of your agreement, so hopefully you won't have any trouble with that. Again, "practice makes perfect", so the process will be easier and quicker each time. There comes a time when you can almost instantly learn a lesson from everything that happens to you. Let me tell you one of my little personal stories. While I lived on the street, I pitied myself many times a day. But in retrospect there was something that did me a lot of good and was my highlight every day. To sleep on the street, we protected ourselves against the cold with cardboard boxes. And I was the only one of the group who owned a cardboard box of a refrigerator. It was so big that I could even stretch out in it.

Whenever I entered my "suite", stored my seven things and the flaps were well closed against the cold, I felt grateful and happy because I had a big cardboard box to sleep in! I even believe that because of these moments of gratitude, Don José appeared and changed my life. Gratitude, alchemy and patience make a great team. Sorry to interrupt, Mary, this little remark was simply necessary. Please continue.

– We've heard that before from you, Joe – this time it's Mary who smiles mischievously.

– Yes, Mary, please go on. And you, waiter, will you please serve us another glass of wine – now I'm taking him in my arms.

– Waiter? I'll show you ... – Joe takes the joke well, but I can't get away without a friendly pat on my shoulder when refilling the glass.

– Jorge, pay attention, because now comes the third and most difficult part of gratitude, namely being grateful for the future – Mary doesn't want to lose the thread of the conversation, for which I am grateful to her, because her last statement makes me incredibly curious.

– Being grateful to the future? How can I be thankful for something that has not yet happened?

– Relax and listen to me carefully. To be thankful for things before they have happened to you has a power that still amazes me daily. Be grateful from the heart for something you wish for, with the same intensity as if it had already happened, and wait and see. I assure you, true miracles have already happened to me for which I still have no explanation.

– And to me! – Joe throws in, flipping through a book.

– Then we're talking about something like magic, I reply a little confused.

– Not really magic, but comparable. I attribute it to the power of the Infinity, as a reward for the gratitude for our gifts. Joe, on the other hand, has a more scientific explanation that sounds wonderful. Joe, I know how much you love this subject, so go ahead.

– Do you realise what a great team we make, Jorge? – Joe asks me after kissing Mary tenderly on the cheek.

– Well, to start with, we humans work like radios.

– What? Joe, I admit you never cease to amaze me. Radios?

– Ha-ha-ha! – my amazement makes us all laugh. It's science, so you'll have no trouble following me. I'm fascinated by quantum physics because its latest discoveries can explain much of what was previously in the realm of the mystical. Physics has proven that everything you perceive are vibrations that our brain converts into colours, smells, tastes, light, matter, water, etc. depending on the frequency. Even you vibrate. And that's where the radio comes in. When you turn the wheel, the station you are listening to changes. You tune it to a specific wave or frequency. This is also how your inner wheel works, which you can turn up or down, which you do unconsciously all the time. Depending on your vibrations, you tune in to situations and people with the same frequency as the radio. With low vibrations like self-pity, the tuned in radio will probably bring less pleasant events, with high vibrations you will attract events and people of the same vibration. As simple as it sounds, we function in a certain way like radios.

– Yes, but how do I manage to set the vibration high?

– You receive and send out your vibrations through feelings. The way you feel, you just vibrate. Just as vibrations are at different frequencies, there are different frequencies or levels of feeling, of joy and peace at one end of the scale and depression and laziness at the other. I have already touched on the meaning of the feelings when I signed the agreement. They are the language of the heart and have the power to resonate with and attract everything that is on the same frequency. We can use our thoughts, which also have their own vibration, to create feelings. But what ultimately attracts one or the other are the feelings. Our problem is not that we lack good feelings, but that we constantly unconsciously create feelings with low vibrations that are automatically sent out and therefore attract events and situations on the same low frequency. Earlier you spoke with Mary about health. For example, it has been scientifically proven that stress is the worst enemy of the immune system. This means that this low vibration, which is so common today, not only makes you feel bad, it also causes many diseases. In network marketing, people wonder why things don't work out the way they want them to. But if you put all their daily feelings into a film, everything would be clear to them immediately. For your personal transformation, you have to adjust the wheel of your radio. This will not be easy, but it is necessary.

– But, Joe, if I'm sad or troubled with debt, how can I feel happy? I don't see how that could work.

– That's difficult, you're right. But at this point, gratitude comes into play again as our best ally. The advantage of this feeling over others such as joy and peace is that it is much easier to bring about consciously and willingly. Deeply felt gratitude will really lead you to joy and peace, just as you have always longed for. And I use the word feel emphatically because it is not enough to think only of gratitude, you must feel it as intensely as you can. When applied to your business, you will attract the right people and situations for your successful development with higher vibrations. In a way, gratitude is a shortcut or trick to get your vibration up faster. In the beginning, it can be very helpful to make a list of all the things you feel thankful for in life and to carry it with you at all times. Read it several times if you notice the attack of any virus trying to dampen your frequency, this way you will feel the gratitude as strongly as possible.

– Sorry to interrupt, Joe. You mean, the gratitude will also help me with any mental viruses you mention?

– Of course, it will. As if it were yesterday, I remember Don José telling me about his ancestors, the mysterious and wise Anasazi people. They had already discovered centuries ago the inner struggle between the true self and the mental viruses mentioned. Some battles you will win, some you will lose, but if you do not even know that you are fighting a battle, you will not fight. Your viruses will make you believe that you are just like that and you will surrender to them. You are now a warrior whose battles are fought in your mind. You must not admit defeat because what is at stake is too important, namely your happiness and, in the extreme, your life. Breathe deeply and rein in yourself, as Don José put it. If necessary, read through your list of gratitude again and again until your vibration has risen far enough and your enemy has been put to flight. Don José said that one must exercise mental discipline for twenty-five hours a day because the viruses are always lurking. From one moment to the next, any misunderstanding can turn into a great destructive emotional drama if we are not careful. Self-pity, depression or stress are among our enemies. They occur more often than one would like to believe.

– And what if I lose the battle, as you call it?

– At this point, you'll lose battles, but you'll see how it goes. With the proper discipline, there will be fewer and fewer, and the battles lost will not be long lasting or particularly dramatic. This afternoon you spoke of upward spirals. There are also downward spirals from which you have to get out as quickly as possible to get back on track. In other words, to raise our vibrational frequency.

– And a deeply felt sense of gratitude is the most effective way to do this – I make a note of that.

– Exactly! Use this power that life offers us as often as possible. Gratitude is a common characteristic of all people who have undergone their personal transformation.

– Gentlemen, I'm enjoying the entertainment, but I'm tired. If you will excuse me, I shall go to bed now – says Mary with a suppressed yawn.

– Yes, I think we'll do that, too. It's been a long and intense day – Joe's joining his wife. What do you think, Jorge?

– Yeah, let's go to bed. I'm tired too.

– Don't forget to say thank you for everything you experienced and learned today – Joe reminds me.

– So much has happened...!

– Ah, one more thing. Mary and I always take a walk in the morning to loosen our limbs and get some oxygen. You don't mind joining us, do you?

– Not at all. I'm sure it's a good start to the day.

– All right. Then I'll meet you in the kitchen at 8:00 sharp for breakfast.

– Eight o'clock? But tomorrow's Sunday...!

– Ha-ha-ha...! You lazy bones. I know it's Sunday, so I'll meet you at eight. On Monday I would have said seven. Besides, it's midnight now, so you have plenty of time to sleep.

– Yeah, but on Sundays...! – I jest.

– On Sundays, what? – Joe almost intimidates me with that penetrating look in his eye.

– No, nothing. I'll see you tomorrow at eight sharp.

– I'll see you at eight sharp tomorrow. Good night, Jorge. Sleep tight, Jorge.

– Good night, you two. I'll see you both tomorrow.

The Magic Fulcrum

At eight o'clock sharp, the delicious smell of freshly baked bread already rises into my nose at the top of the stairs and literally makes my mouth water.

– Good morning! It smells supernaturally good.

– Good morning, Jorge! It smells like the corn bread that Mary bakes. With a little olive oil, it's a real delicacy. Come and taste it – Joe asks me and waves me over to the table.

Everything tastes wonderful. After a few cups of green tea and several motivation videos on Mary's laptop, which charge me with positive energy, we are well prepared for the walk. This time we choose the way to the lake. After a few meters I realise, due to our speed, that this should be anything but a walk.

– Listen, you guys are going pretty fast. Are you in a hurry?

– Are you that lazy again? Let's go. You should be able to keep up with both of us old folks. Ha-ha-ha...! – they laugh at me and look at each other like two youngsters fresh in love.

– Fair enough, I thought this was going to be a walk – I get used to it, so I keep quiet and concentrate on the path so as not to stumble.

With the singing of the birds as the only acoustic background, we hurry on in silence at a speed I can hardly keep up. For their age, they are in incredibly good shape. Mary notices my breathlessness and kindly offers me a water bottle, which I accept and empty immediately. Because of the short drinking break I have to run after them to catch up with them. I find it increasingly difficult to keep up with them. Obviously, I am totally out of shape and make a fool of myself again. A feeling of shame comes over me.

After about forty minutes we finally get back to the house. Totally exhausted I sit down on the veranda. While I take a deep breath to get my breath back, Joe takes a seat next to me.

– I see you should work on your fitness, Jorge – he advises me and hands me a glass of fresh lemonade, which tastes wonderful.

– I was just thinking the same thing.

– Yesterday I told you I was going to talk about habits today. I didn't realise how urgent it was. Ha-ha ha!

– Show a little mercy, Joe. I blame him for his lack of understanding.

– I'm sorry, Jorge. Please, don't be angry. Let's take a shower, it'll refresh you, so we can continue afterwards.

– Thanks, Joe.

After a soothing shower, Mary invites me into the library. There I find Joe over papers spread out on the billiard table. Up close, I can make out what appear to be old maps.

– Planning a trip, Joe?

– My dear friend, every day of my life is a journey! But today is not about traveling, I want to make you understand something with these cards. Please pay attention now, because we're going to talk about basic topics.

– Go ahead, Joe, we're ready to go – I answer and get ready to write everything down in detail.

– As I told you yesterday, Jorge, in order to achieve all the really worthwhile goals or successes in life, you have to approach certain things in a certain way and give up others. I am talking about changing both our mental and physical habits, both in business and in life in general. I also talked about our brain being on autopilot most of the day. The habits are the same as you have acquired them. We humans are creatures of habit, there is no way to change that. But what you can change are the habits themselves. If you adopt the right behaviours and stop the wrong ones, you can create whatever you set out to do. Strangely enough, many people make vain attempts to change their patterns. They choose to do sports and don't do them, they want to be more consistent and can't get it right, or they want to earn more and don't do anything about it. They may start out well in the first week, but then months pass before they even remember their goal.

– It is anything but easy. It seems to me that habits are stuck deep inside us. What you are talking about, I have experienced enough of myself already.

– Yes, especially on the first of January! – he laughs. – Everybody in the world makes good intentions to change their behaviour on that day, and a week later hardly anyone thinks about it anymore. All because people are going about it the wrong way.

– What do you mean by wrong?

– They don't really get to the bottom of the problem. Let me tell you another story from my private fund. As you may have noticed, we're a non-smoking household.

– Of course, I've noticed that. If you did smoke, you wouldn't be in such good shape.

– Well, as I stand before you, I was once a smoker. Don José was very annoyed with me, but that habit had me firmly in its grip. However hard I tried, I could not get away from it. I tried all kinds of methods, but before I knew what was happening to me, I was already about to light my next cigarette. This cursed habit was also the reason for my regular quarrels with Mary. But one day something amazing happened to me: in less than five seconds a doctor made sure that the vice was driven out!

– In less than five seconds? That's impossible. Well, tell me. – I'm bursting with curiosity.

– One short sentence was enough to chase my vice away.

– A single sentence? Was it a hypnotist?

– Not at all, I was fully conscious the whole time.

– So, what is this incredibly powerful phrase, Joe?

– The doctor told me, "You have lung cancer. " – I'm at a loss for words and I don't quite know what to say.

– But... well... I'm sorry, Joe. You're all right now, aren't you?

– Yes, thank you, I'm done with the treatment. I owe my recovery to the doctors – and to Mary, who made me go to the examination. It wasn't easy, but in the end, it turned out to be an alchemical transformation, because not only did I quit smoking from one day to the next, but I also began to pay much more attention to my health. This means that at the same time, I changed other harmful habits, not just smoking. Almost imperceptibly, I began to eat better and to take more exercise. Even if it may sound strange, the news certainly saved my life. It forced me to undergo an alchemical transformation of my body. Today I am twenty years older, but I feel much better than before.

– Once again alchemy comes into play.

– That's life, better you remember that. You are probably wondering now what all this has to do with your business.

– Yes, I'm dying to know.

– Then pay attention, because here comes the most important point! – he keeps his eyes on me and he goes on... Do you know what a fulcrum is?

– A fulcrum? I don't know, Joe. Once again, I look stupid.

– It's the technical name for what we colloquially call the "point of support " for a lever. I've introduced you to the magic levers to help you get the most out of your business, but as you know, each lever needs a point of contact to grip. Otherwise, it remains just an iron bar.

– Yeah, right.

– So, write down the explanation. The Magic Fulcrum is "Find your Motivaction".

– Sorry, Joe, I think I heard wrong. You said "motivation", didn't you?

— Ha-ha-ha! No, I think there's nothing wrong with your ears. I said "Motivaction" with a "c".

— Motivaction! I've never heard that word before.

— It's a word Don José created by combining the words "motivation" and "action". This means that the motivaction is the motivation that inevitably pushes you to the right action. It is not an ordinary motivation, because it immediately changes your habits. It represents the "why" to implement necessary behavioural changes that will lead you to a concrete goal. To achieve any goal, you must know beforehand why you want to implement it, otherwise you will not make the necessary efforts and habit changes.

My motivaction to give up smoking was delivered to me by my doctor with the sentence mentioned. From one moment to the next I stopped! Then I realised that what Don José preached to me over and over again was absolutely true. The powerful and deceitful habits lose their power when you find your true motivaction. It leads you to take the necessary actions to achieve your goal. Without a point of contact, without a fulcrum, a lever is almost useless, and this is what happens to our magic levers.

If you do not find your true motivaction, they serve little purpose, and you will not be able to change a habit permanently. You remain on the surface, but your true motivaction is hidden deep inside. As always, this requires unsparing honesty with yourself. Over the years, you may see other, perhaps even greater motivactions appear within you, but the one you are encountering now must drive tears into your eyes with emotion when you think of them. For they will shake you up and bring about a change in your habits, almost without you noticing. Don José always said that there are two particularly memorable days in life, that of birth and that of discovering your motivaction. Without them, everything is difficult and tedious. It is through them that you become a proactive person, that is, you will not care if it rains, if you are embarrassed or if you only get a few hours of sleep. All this will fade into the background once you have found your true motivaction. Proactive means acting on the basis of values to which your motivaction is closely related. Dive deeply into your personal principles and values, and you will find what you are looking for. Many people want to be proactive because they have read about it in some book, but they won't get very far without the motivaction.

– I read a book about proactivity, and on paper it worked wonderfully, but I got it the way you described it. In my everyday life, nothing has changed at all.

– Don't worry, that's the rule. First and foremost, you have to find your point of contact, your why, to take advantage of all the levers of the business and your full potential. This can't be done in five minutes, because it requires a review of your true principles and values. Money in itself is nobody's motivaction, but merely a consequence of it. The motivaction lies in the realm of "feeling", not in that of "having". As I said, it must stir you up. What drives people to make important decisions are feelings. For example, how would you react if I told you that I would give you a brand new car when you climbed Mount Everest tomorrow?

– That you're crazy! Of course, I'd say no, even if you offered me two cars. When I almost fainted on a march less than an hour ago.

– But what if I told you that Sara's life and that of your family depends on herbs that only grow up there, and you're the only one who can get them?

– Well, then I wouldn't think twice about it and try – I reply, after I got goose bumps just thinking about it.

– Can you tell the difference? A car is not enough motivation for you to risk your life, it does not create the necessary emotion in you to make this huge effort. It's quite different when it comes to something as elementary as the life of your family.

– Yes, of course, but this example does not help me.

– Why not?

– Well, because it's too extreme. Who wouldn't risk his life to save his family from disaster?

– That's easy. All those who don't know that their families' lives are in danger. Like you, for example.

– Like me? My family is not in danger.

– Didn't you tell us that your financial situation prevented you from having children? Your child couldn't be born yet because of your economic bondage. So, you think your family is not in danger?

– Well, in that sense... – Joe's objection, which is as strong as it is accurate, troubles me.

– Forgive my directness, but there is no other way. In your case, it's easy to see with this small, yet so far-reaching detail. But in one form or another almost everyone is enslaved. There is no extra entrance fee at stake. The price is freedom and the balance between quality time and money. As long as you do not have financial freedom, you will not really be free. Does it seem to you to be too small a motive to gain freedom for yourself and your family? Therefore, everything depends on the size of your "why", i. e. your motivaction. Find answers to "how", "why" and "where to". The motivaction provides the answer to "why", and the system of levers and traps provides the answer to "how".

– And the answer to "where to"? You haven't explained that.

He grabs me by the shoulder and points to the maps on the billiard table.

– What if you want to get to Barcelona on foot from Madrid, but change your route every day?

– I'd probably never get there.

– Right. Ideally, you'd take the same direction every day, so the journey wouldn't be endless. Otherwise, you would either never arrive or you would arrive much later. The former is more likely, because with the second option you would probably lose motivation halfway through and give up because you haven't seen your destination for too long. The same can be applied to the business or all kinds of other projects. I suppose you have heard of the power of focus. Focusing on a single goal will get you there sooner or later. But if you realign the direction two or three times, you will get nowhere. Focusing means constantly following the same route until you reach your destination. Some days you will progress further, others less. You may lose your way in between and lose some time until you are back on course. Don't worry about that, that's the way it works. Adversity can force you to the ground temporarily, but the trick is to get up once more when you fall. I can see Don José's face when we talked about focus. He looked directly at me and said: "My son, don't do things by halves". Your motivaction also helps you to find the right focus. Otherwise, you would quickly lose focus with any distraction or with a newer project that you would sooner or later replace with another one. You would go round in circles and end up at the same point over and over again. The best way to reach your goal is the straight path. Seneca already knew: "If you don't know the harbour you want to sail into, no wind is the right one for you."

– Then the "where to" is a mixture of the goals and the focus.

– Exactly! On the one hand, you should know where you are going, i. e. know your goal, on the other hand you should keep your direction, i. e. focus. However, if you don't know why you want to arrive, none of what we have discussed will help you on your journey. The motivaction will give you the strength you need when you think you have none left, it will drive you to do unpleasant things, it will cover your ears when some gossip wants to tear down your project, and it will support you in your personal and corporate metamorphosis. Without a convincing motive, why would you make the effort to walk the 600 kilometres between Madrid and Barcelona? If you have an appropriately significant and emotional motive, you will wake up every day thinking only of walking. So, it will unconsciously become a new habit.

– So, a change of habit is a direct result of the motivaction?

– Habits are changed by action and effort, you are only able to change habits if you want to reach your goal. It is about mental as well as physical habits. Do you think that in winter, at seven o'clock in the morning, I wouldn't rather stay in a cuddly warm bed than leave?

– I suppose so.

– It's true, but the extent of my motivaction, namely to maintain my health, is greater than the desire to stay in the warm. Again, it is a very special kind of motivation that inevitably spurs you on to action. To come to the point of the cards laid out here: Yesterday, in our conversation, you told me you'd read enough books on network marketing to know that it didn't make a difference. I assume that you are already trying to understand why that was so.

– Sure, I didn't really understand them. In the books I read, everything seemed to me to be much more complicated than with your examples.

– The problem with the hundreds or thousands of books on the market, among which there are also really good ones, is that it is very easy to fall into another trap.

– The fifth trap? Let's hear it, Joe.

– I see you keep count. I think that's very commendable. The Fifth Fatal Trap is "Become a Cartographer".

– What? A cartographer! Now I'm really at a loss. I'm curious how you'll explain it to me.

– It's simple. – He reaches for one of the world maps on the pool table and hands it to me – Mark on the map a place you would like to travel to.

– Done – I paint Paris because I owe this trip to Sara.

– Paris? Good choice. Now focus, and ask the map to take you to Paris.

– What? Are you in the mood for another joke? – just by looking at it, he makes me want to keep following his instructions – How can I ask the map to do that? It can't take me anywhere.

– Exactly! The map on its own will not take you anywhere. So, if the map can't take you, how will you get to Paris?

– Well, since I don't have a car, I'll have to walk.

– Ha, ha, ha ... Forgive me – when he notices my sour face, he underlines his apology with folded hands. – Right, let's get on with it. Since the map can't take you there, it seems you have to get there under your own steam.

– In my case without a car, yes – again there is a smile on Joe's lips that slowly drives me crazy.

– You know, Jorge, in all these years I have seen many people who, at the beginning of their network marketing activities, read vast amounts of books on the subject, but without tangible and lasting results. Without realising it, they have become theorists, i. e. cartographers of network marketing.

– But Joe, reading can never damage. I have learned many interesting things from books.

– Of course, reading is a positive thing. Just take a look, then you know I've read hundreds of books. I love to read. It becomes a problem when you become a theorist, a cartographer. The successful opposite is the quality of the discoverer. The cartographer resembles a "commentator" in many ways, while the discoverer is a "doer", and you know my opinion on that. Find your motivaction and you will immediately become an explorer in search of your treasure, namely a life full of meaning. The highest good is a life worth living. The cartographers who stay in the office will not get any refusals and will have it warmer, but you will feel much more alive. And that's what a great life is all about, remember?

– I promise to be ruthlessly honest with myself to track down my motivaction.

– I see you've got this whole thing figured out to perfection. I'm glad. Congratulations.

– Thanks, Joe. But I still have a long way to go.

– Yes, there is. And speaking of walking, I'd like to get back to your lousy form.

– Oh, Joe… You really think it's that bad?

– The fact is, you couldn't keep up with two old people. If you want to believe you're in shape, that's your problem. Maybe you'd rather hear a magic phrase from a doctor, like me, to start taking care of yourself.

– No, thank you.

– You can never stress enough the importance of regular exercise. It's enough to walk briskly for twenty or thirty minutes a day. You need to work up a little sweat, my friend. Don José always said that if I didn't spend part of my time and money on keeping my body healthy, I would give both to doctors and hospitals. But I remained very stubborn on this subject. Leaving in the morning was out of the question for me. I preferred to read a book or prepare for some workshop. I considered exercise a waste of time. With this lifestyle as a smoker and without sports, my days were numbered. That is why I told you that this news saved my life, just like you did later. If you dedicate a certain amount of time each day to your physical health, your relationship with your body will change. I don't think many people speak to their heart, kidneys or lungs the way I do.

– So, you talk to your kidneys?

– Well, rather than talking to them, I often thank them for

their selfless full-time work. If this makes me seem a little crazy to you, I want to tell you that I also thank the more than a hundred trillion cells in my body that keep me alive thanks to perfectly coordinated work. And also for the fact that nothing hurts me, or at least almost nothing. In return, the best way to do this is to do this movement, which supplies my body with oxygen so that the cells can breathe properly. But sport has the most beneficial effect on the brain. It works more clearly and you are in a better mood. All of these things together put you in the right mood to tackle the challenges ahead. And the right attitude will also help you to recognise and destroy attacking mental viruses. Once you get used to it, you can hardly do without the morning march.

– I really have to pull myself together. I haven't really done any sport for a long time, although after the initial exhaustion I am now feeling great.

– You see? Physical exercise gives you a feeling of well-being almost immediately, and for free. Although in terms of health, the mere motive of not falling ill should be enough for certain changes, such as regular exercise, you will manage this change and many other habit changes almost by yourself once you have found your true motivaction. If you don't find it, all current habits will tend to return and settle down. I went alone with a tent into the mountains to find my motivaction.

– Are you asking me to go alone into the mountains to camp?

– No, you have to find your own way to find them. Without doubt, however, being alone is a great way to get inside yourself.

– The enlightening loneliness!

– Enlightening loneliness? I told you, you have a talent for giving things a name. I like that term very much. May I use it in the future?

– Sure, Joe, go ahead.

– Or better yet, I'll give you something else in return.

– Something else? Something else what?

– Do you trust me?

– Absolutely, Joe.

– Then run upstairs and leave the house through the main entrance.

– You want me to leave the house?

– You might end up with a real ear problem. Ha-ha-ha!

– All right, I'll be on my way. What kind of surprise have you got for me now? – as I'm walking past him, he gives me a gentle nudge, like to give me a little speed.

I'm climbing the library steps and heading for the front door. Mary looks at me with a strange smile. I have no idea what's going on, but I'd like to know.

– Mary, what are you doing?

– Go outside and you'll see.

I open the door and step outside. A beautiful, spotlessly polished blue car is parked a few yards from the porch. I keep an eye out for Tom, because we might have to drive the car somewhere, but I don't see him. On the windshield, I notice something that looks like a postcard. I go down the steps and see what it is. When I reach the car, I read the following text: "Thank you for saving my life. It is the least I can do. Mary has the keys."

– What? I'm not quite sure what this is all about. Looking around, I see Mary looking in my direction, waving a bunch of keys.

– Are you going to get your keys or not? – Mary makes the keys jingle.

– My keys? It's for me? – Joe comes out, grabs Mary around the shoulder, and they're both smiling at me

– I don't believe it. No, I can't accept it. It's too much.

– It's too much? Did you read the card? You risked your life to save mine. This is nothing compared to what you gave me that night. On top of everything else, I destroyed yours, so you can't say no. You should also remember the tenth part of your agreement. Signed is signed, sorry. There's no turning back. You should start it now and test it. – he can just say before I jump on them and hug them.

– Wait a minute! That's why you laughed earlier when I was annoyed about the car comment? – now it all makes sense. And I was about to get seriously pissed at Joe for what he said.

Joe shrugs, which is a sign of approval.

– Well, excuse me, Joe.

– It's all right. No worries.

– Come on, let's take a test drive together – I invite them in when I open the car door.

We climb into the car, same model as mine, only in the latest version. As my car had been on the road for fifteen years, the only noticeable similarity is in the model name. It has all the technological extras you can imagine.

– I will have to read the manual – I announce excitedly.

– Yes, but you will also have to steer. Ha-ha-ha! – we look at each other and have to laugh at the thought of the conversation about cartographers and explorers.

– Are we ready to go? – like a little kid, I get impatient to start this jewel.

– Wait, there's someone missing – Mary thinks.

– Will Tom be joining us? – I ask around, and then I press my head.

– Look around you, Jorge – I hear Mary's voice again.

I lift my eyes from the dashboard and recognise a silhouette next to the house. Against the sun and through the shadow of the house I cannot see who it is. The person approaches, and to my surprise...

– Sara? But...? How this ...?

I look back and forth between Mary and Joe, smiling to themselves. I never forget that smile.

– Thank you, Mary, thank you, Joe – I say just before I open the car door and fall around Sara's neck.

– But Sara... What about dinner at your parents'?

– Well, sometimes you have to prioritise – she answers with a smile. – I discussed it with them. It's all right, we'll visit them another time.

– Come on, you lovebirds, let's test this car! Ha, ha, ha ...! – Joe from inside the car is pushing us to hurry.

Sara and I get in, and while I enjoy the pleasurable ride on the roads around the estate, I listen to the story of how Mary prepared the surprise for me.

On my return, I take a closer look at the stylish shape of my new car. At the rear, something catches my eye that should not be there. On the metallic lacquer of the tailgate, next to my mobile phone number, there is a lettering with the following words:

"If you're looking for a way to make your life better, call me."

– What is this, Joe, another one of your jokes?

– Ha-ha-ha! No, this is serious. If you want the present, you have to take it as it is. You don't like the font, or you got a problem with the colour?

– No, I don't mean the colour or the letters. It's the writing itself. It's kind of destroying the aesthetics of the car, don't you think?

– Aesthetics? Now you care about aesthetics? Let me tell you something important: To get where you want to go, you have to use every means at your disposal. All business owners do. The car is just one of many resources besides your contacts, your money, your time or your house. When you focus all your energy on one goal, you put everything you have, and often everything you don't have, at the service of the cause. This small, elegant lettering with your phone number will not only work for you, but possibly also bring your best partner into the business. Remember, people need to know that you have something to offer. You have to go all the way, Jorge! What's at stake is too important to worry about the aesthetics of your car. Besides, you should be proud of your project when you show yourself to the world. The inscription will make you look confident about what you're offering.

– I doubt if it'll do much good, Joe.

– You know what happens to water when you heat it up to 99 degrees?

– What about it? I don't know what you're getting at, Joe.

– Water heated to 99 degrees is just hot water. But only one more degree and it starts to boil and evaporate. With that steam, you could power an engine that weighs a ton. The difference is only one degree. I want to make you understand that small details often have a big effect that makes the difference. Never lose sight of the details. Ten years from now, this subtle inscription may not have been of any use, or it may have changed the lives of hundreds or even thousands of people, including you. Wouldn't you like to try it?

– In any case, I don't think it will damage me. And on second thought, the lettering doesn't disturb the aesthetics too much either. The design is very stylish. Thank you, Joe, for thinking of such details and opening my eyes to so much.

– You're welcome, it was my pleasure. But always remember that you must put all your resources into the service of your dreams and not the other way around. It is paradoxical how carelessly people give up their dreams for a supposedly safe life full of resources that are not in the least bit profitable. There are people who have built and run highly profitable businesses on the Internet with the help of a mobile phone, just like your one. We are talking about the same mobile phone that others only use to make phone calls or send messages. What you get out of your resources is up to you. One of Don José's favourite sayings was: "God deals cards to everyone, but you decide how you play the game".

– Interesting saying. Don José was a very wise man.

– Indeed, he was. And on the subject of how to make the most of your resources, I'd like to take this appropriate opportunity to offer a few more tips that may seem logical, but are by no means. I want you to understand the difference between an expense and an investment.

– Oh, Joe, I studied economics! – I interject with a slight indignant undertone, since he does not take into account my academic background.

– I know, but if the difference is so clear to you, why spend your life helping to make someone else's dreams come true, instead of using your resources and time to provide a passive income for a quality of life you deserve?

– Um...! – once again, words fail me.

– With the right focus and the right results, you will see all the time and resources you spend on your business as an investment. However, if you are not properly focused, and as an inevitable consequence you do not achieve tangible results, you will see everything as an expense. In both cases, you will be right. The only difference between an expense and an investment is in achieving results. From now on, consider all these resources clearly as the best possible investment to change your life for the better. One of the most striking advantages of network marketing is that it does not require as much economic investment as traditional companies. And as I mentioned earlier about the super benefits, it's a matter of a few months if you do it right. Because the revenues will cover the investments very quickly. So I am talking more about invested time and work. Until you can leave your job, you will have to spend what you consider your free time on this, and that can be tough. Even if it is only temporary, you must always remember that you are investing your time to create something that will contribute to the happiness of your family. The same applies to the question of money. Remember, it's always about investment, not spending.

– No pain, no gain, right?

– Ha-ha-ha! That's it, Jorge! Now let's give the women a hand and set the table.

– Yeah, sure! – I answer and can hardly take my eyes off the huge gift I've just received.

The Immortals

After another wonderful meal prepared by Mary, the women suggest a walk on the estate, and we men, as role model partners, gladly agree. Sara would like to get to know the area around the house better, because on her first visit she did not see much of it.

Just as we are about to leave the house, the phone rings and Mary apologises to take the call. In the meantime, we chat with Joe about how they came across the country house until Mary calls him from the first floor.

– I'm coming, Mary! – Joe answers on the way to the stairs.

After a few minutes the two return hand in hand. There's something wrong with their expressions, as if they'd received some bad news. On top of that, Mary has teary-eyed eyes, whereas Joe seems more calmly.

– Are you Ok? – I ask honestly concerned.

– Yeah, don't worry, Jorge. The challenges of life. Listen, maybe we men should stay here while you women explore the estate? Some important things have occurred to me to discuss with Jorge before you go home – suggests Joe and kisses Mary on the cheek.

– All right - Sara and Mary agree in unison. They seem more and more familiar with each other. Mary is a woman with lots of life experience and can give Sara a lot of good advice.

After the two of them have left, Joe tells me to follow him upstairs to his office. As I enter, I look again at the photos, honours and awards on the wall. Among them I notice a hand-written page, framed in a magnificent frame, which I have never seen before. Up close I recognise the same agreement that Joe had me sign.

– You see, I was telling the truth – Joe interrupts my arbitrary explorations – This is the document Don José had me sign before he took me under his wing. It's practically identical to yours.

– Some things seem to remain unchanged over the years.

– Yes, and I advise you to do the same and frame your agreement. Pick a high-profile spot in your house. But sit down now, Jorge – he's assigning me the same chair at his desk as always.

– I love your study. It's so authentic.

– But you don't know all the details yet.

– What do you mean, not all the details?

– We'll get to that in a minute, because that's what we're here for. Before we do that, I'd like to remind you that this subject is socially taboo. But it will be a great help to you in your search for your true motive. I put the emphasis on "true" because some people believe to have found it after only five minutes. This is doomed to failure from the outset because they only move on the surface. People do not go into themselves with unsparing honesty. And to enter into dialogue with yourself in this absolute honesty, you will do well not to fall into the "Sixth Fatal Trap".

– Give me a piece of paper, I don't have my notebook.

– Forget the notebook now, you can write it down later. Just listen to me carefully. This trap applies to business and life in all its aspects. To recognise and avoid it is one of the most important tasks in your life.

– Tell me about it, Joe. I'm curious what it is.

– "To believe in your immortality" is the sixth fatal trap.

– What? Immortal? Oh, Joe, some crazy man may think he's immortal, but I certainly don't.

– Ha-ha-ha! Well, I'm sorry to inform you that you feel immortal right now. That's all right. Most people do, and you're no exception. At least you're on your way to another consciousness. So, you think you know you're gonna die eventually, right?

– Of course, I know, Joe.

– You think you know it, but the way you live proves otherwise.

– You want my life to prove I don't know my own mortality? Are you crazy, Joe?

– Fortunately, not yet, I hope. Ha-ha-ha! Look, people know in their minds that they're going to die, but few have experienced death at close quarters. The latter, however, have usually changed their attitude towards life from the ground up. They no longer postpone important things because the breath of death has come very close to them. They carry the awareness within them that life is short, even if you live to be ninety or a hundred years old. The point is, soon you will no longer have to be ashamed of what anybody thinks of you, because you will no longer exist. Life does not last forever, my friend.

– Jeez, Joe, I'm sure this triggers something in people who have had concrete experiences with death, but that's not why I should know I'm going to die?

– Your heart doesn't know, only your mind does, and it's not the same thing. I myself have been very close to death, even several times. The last time I landed on you. Have you ever thought seriously about what happened that day? You escaped death by 1/10th of a second, Jorge, imagine that. To internalise this experience will provide you with the key.

– What key?

– The key to life. In the many years I have been living, I have realised how closely life is interwoven with death. Our society tends to see death as something very bad that is better left unsaid. However, it is death that gives life all its meaning. Logically, we should do everything we can to ensure a long life. And it is the awareness of having to die sometime, no matter when, helps you to feel really alive. There is nothing negative about dying, it is just inevitable. The bad thing is not to have lived and not to have used the short time available to us on earth in the best possible way. You should face your mortality every day. You will recognise the 'immortals' by the fact that they always lack something for their happiness, they are not grateful for what they have, and almost always know something that disturbs them. When it rains, the damp weather annoys them, and when the sun shines, they complain about the heat. They have forgotten how to be amazed, and it is difficult for a smile to come over their lips. They are usually people who suffer from the destructive "deferral" disease. They postpone all kinds of important things because they think they have all the time in the world. Usually they prioritise according to urgency rather than importance. And so, their life passes without them noticing the approaching end, until it is too late and there is no way back. Strangely enough, these people also always think they will live to be ninety or a hundred years old. They do not realise that it could be any time. Don José taught me that we should live our lives with the thought that at any moment death could grab us by the shoulder and take everything we think we have. And by everything, I mean everything. A nurse friend of mine who worked in palliative care once told me that dying people do not usually complain about their mistakes in life, but about their failures. "Immortals" won't talk openly about death either. In the wisdom of Don José's ancestors, death is the best guide for the living. It acts as a teacher, guiding us to live life with enthusiasm. Look what it says up there.

He points his finger at a shelf with photos and a kind of vase in between. I rise to see better because I don't know exactly what he means. But even up close I can't see anything remarkable.

– Are you talking about one of the photos, Joe?

– In the middle, between the pictures.

– The vase?

– The vase? Ha-ha-ha! Take the "vase", and read the inscription.

I reach for it and discover a small metal plate with writing on it. When I read it, a shiver goes through my whole body and my heart contracts.

– What do you mean, "Inside here are the ashes of Joseph Goodman. Rest in peace"? What's that? An urn?

– Yes, that is my urn – he calmly explains. – I keep it in sight so it reminds me where I'll be in not too long from now. It's a bit radical, admittedly, but incredibly effective, I can assure you. So, I never forget to give Mary as many kisses as possible, laugh as often as I can, and live each moment as if it were my last. Our days are very limited, so each awakening represents something special and unique. Even if there are still so many days ahead of you, there are always too few. Since you have studied economics, you will probably know what happens to the price of something that is lacking, right?

– I think you mean that the price rises when there is a shortage.

– Exactly! And I can assure you, the rarest asset of any man is the days he has left. That's why every day that is really lived can be weighed in gold. Moreover, the feeling of being mortal will support your discussed transformation in an invaluable way. This awareness will help you to risk everything you are in order to become who you can be, much like the caterpillar. All this is what the urn here reminds me of every day, in case I am tempted to forget. I advise you to do the same.

– That seems a little macabre, Joe.

– See how you still feel immortal? You'll soon change your mind, or so I hope. Take it from someone who hasn't got too many days left to live, in the strictest possible sense.

– Don't say that, Joe.

– Well, it's the truth. It is also true that you don't have as many as you think, ha, ha, ha...! Need I remind you again that you almost died when our two lives crossed? Use this experience to feel death and absorb its teachings. Nothing happens without a reason. There are always lessons in the most urgent events of your life. Do not see it as an accident, but as an opportunity to apply alchemy to the value of your life. Turn days spent routinely and perceived as a struggle for survival into gifts to develop and enjoy life to the full. Now do you understand why I begin each morning by sitting up in bed to thank the Infinity for the new day?

– From this perspective...

– With a whole new relationship to death and an awareness of your "expiration date", you will find your true motivaction much easier. It will also make it much easier for you to enjoy every moment of your life. I guess you could put it like that: If you stop feeling immortal, you will never be bored again. I enjoy it very much, or rather I feel very sorry when I hear someone say they are doing something "to kill time". More than that, these people are wasting their time. They think they are immortal and assume that they have so much time at their disposal that they have to "kill" it in order not to get bored. "Killing time" is a clear sign of "immortality". Some mental virus wants to keep us from developing an awareness of the limited duration of our lives. It wants to prevent us from changing our lives radically because it wants to keep us fearful.

– Frightened? Why?

– Because fear blocks us and we shy away from the necessary risks that will allow us to live a great life. When we are scared, we fall victim to all kinds of fears that advise us to stay the way we are. And this is where the inner conflict arises between who you are and who you would like to be. This inner conflict and the resulting suffering are the reward for the respective virus. That's how it won the battle. If you admit to yourself that your existence is of infinitesimal short duration, you bring with you the awareness that every moment is unique and you will be happier with every day. For you will stop being blocked by so many, often unfounded, worries and begin to properly deal with the challenges of each day. Challenges because you will no longer face problems, but challenges. And once again, thanks to alchemy, you will turn these challenges into teachers. The vast majority of viruses require you to suffer in order to survive. Therefore, their existence becomes superfluous and the annoying virus will disappear.

– Where you are addressing these mental viruses, let me ask you a question about it. Are they to blame every time I get angry?

– Of course. Besides, something very strange happens to them when we are upset. Let me see if I can find anything. Ah, here it is! – Joe takes a little glass bottle out of a box – Let's go downstairs and I'll show you how Don José explained this to me.

We descend the stairs, leave the house and go to a pool

between thick bushes that acts as a rainwater reservoir. Up close, I am surprised to see that it is filled almost to the brim and colourful fish swim in it. Because of the remains of an old diving board I assume that it was used as a swimming pool in former times.

– What do you think happens if I let a single drop of black ink drip into this pool – Joe questions me and takes the bottle out of his pocket.

– Just one drop? I don't think it would really change anything.

– Let's try it! – Joe stretches his arm across the water with the ink-filled pipette. He squeezes and a black drop falls into the water. An initially visible black veil quickly disappears into the thousands of litres of water in the pool.

– Nothing happened, right? – I notice curiously.

– Right, nothing happened. The water in the basin is still clear.

– I can see that myself, Joe. Once again, I'm not sure I follow you.

– You asked me if your trouble had to do with the mental viruses.

– Yes, but how does my question relate to that?

– Imagine that the problem that caused your anger at any given moment was like the drop of ink, and the pool is the same as your life. As we have found, a single drop of ink, however black it may be, cannot cloud clear water because there is much more of it, and the ink dissolves. However, when you get angry, exactly the opposite happens. A single drop, a single problem, manages to darken your entire being comprehensively. Your inner pool becomes so cloudy that all the good in your life temporarily disappears. A single difficulty should not make us forget all that is positive, but the virus transforms this drop of ink, that singular problem, into effective ink that colours everything black. And the worst thing about it is that when you get angry, you often say and do things that make the situation even worse instead of looking for a solution. You simply lose control over the words and open the door to all kinds of feelings of remorse and guilt that follow us everywhere. In a moment of inner darkness, we can do great harm and inflict it upon ourselves. If we remember all the good things in our life, the clear water of our inner pools, and are grateful for them, we would make the work of the respective virus much more difficult. Life is full of challenges that we have to face every day, but it is up to us whether a virus can completely cloud our inner pool or whether a problem dissolves like a drop of ink.

– These damn mental viruses! And how can I tell if my thoughts are infected or not?

– That is what experience will teach you, but for a start I can give you a scent to locate viruses.

– Yes, please, I'm listening.

– They always appear in connection with problems that don't really exist.

– What do you mean, problems that don't exist?

– Ha-ha-ha! Well, that they don't exist.

– Why should I feel bad about something that doesn't exist, Joe?

– It happens to you all the time. Not just to you, but to the majority of people.

– Please explain it to me in more detail, Joe – on this point, I'm taking out my pencil to write down the answer to this new riddle.

– Look, Jorge, you can detect infected thoughts by always referring to the past or the future. Colloquially, I guess we'd call them guilty conscience or worry. Almost everyone is constantly carrying around worries due to negative mental projections of assumed future problems that will probably never materialise. They form a kind of virtual reality that exists only in their heads. They worry so much that they often end up not caring about the matter in question at all. As Don José said: "The analysis of analysis produces paralysis". If you analyse it in depth, you will find that it makes no sense at all. Worries are thoughts contaminated by acquired fears, that is, mental viruses.

– All well and good. Worries do not exist because nothing has happened yet. But you have a bad conscience because of things that have actually happened.

– These happened in their own time.

– What does that mean?

– It means now they only exist in your head. When it's a problem with someone else, the person concerned may not even remember it. And if they do, in a different way to you. So, what is the truth? Yours, theirs or none of them?

– My goodness, it must be a mixture of the two.

– Ha-ha-ha! I wish you felt that way about all your guilt. Then you'd automatically be happier. But I'm going for the third option, which is none of them. Our memory is more forgetful than we think. However, the brain is able to create a proper film of events based on individual memories. And of course, the virus responsible takes care that you always appear in it as someone's victim or tormentor. There are friends and even siblings who haven't spoken to each other for years, but apart from a vague memory they hardly know what really happened. And the resentment, which also belongs to the same group of infected thoughts, persists, and they even take it to their grave. Many people carry an incredible burden because they cannot apologise or forgive.

I can immediately think of a few friends that I have practically lost sight of because of problems that I don't even remember!

– But Joe, how can I free myself from all this?

– It is arduous work, but the alchemy of forgiveness and thanksgiving is a wonderful way to begin.

– All right, I'll try to pay attention to that.

– Don't worry, with a little patience you will soon begin to locate them and ignore them. For now, try not to take everything so dead serious and enjoy the moment, the now.

– So, there are no viruses in the present, Joe?

– No, they don't have power here. But it's not so easy to sink completely into the now. If you do, you are at peace with yourself, because you are aware that the present is what it is. The expectation that it should be different is at the root of human suffering. You can make an effort in your life to improve any aspect, but the present moment, your life in this very moment, is what it is. Not accepting your life as it is becomes a dead end, primarily because that's the way it is. In order to reach this insight, the consciousness of being mortal and not immortal will help you tremendously. The feeling of mortality is the most effective antidote to virus-infested thoughts.

It makes me think. I have the feeling that I have read about this subject in some book, but have not given it the appropriate attention.

– Write down the words written in this silver-plated frame under the shelf.

– Where? In this one?

– Ha, ha, ha...! All I see is one silver frame, Jorge.

– Fair enough.

I concentrate on the text and write it down, while the wisdom contained within impresses me deeply.

PRAYER FOR SERENITY

God, give me the serenity
to accept things I cannot change,
the courage to change things I can change,
and the wisdom to know the difference.

– Very wise words, Joe. Did you write them?

– No, they were written by Francis of Assisi. They are also always across from my desk. St Francis was very inspired when he wrote them, and at the same time they're based on pure common sense. They will help you to fight all the pangs of conscience and worries that afflict you.

– I will always remember them, Joe.

– I hope so. It would be very good news for your life. By the way, did you bring the keys to your new car?

– Here they are – I pull the keys out of my pocket.

– Well, let's get going. I want to take you to a special place.

– Won't the women be upset?

– Never mind, I've already told Mary. I've also asked her to discuss with Sara the process ahead of her, the process of building your network marketing business by your side. She's been through this phase, too. Did you know that I met Mary a day later as Don José?

– The very next day! There you can see that you were heard loud and clear from the infinite on that cliff.

– That's right. These days were marked by profound changes. It is incredible how a few days can completely change a life. And Mary could not understand this world at first either, so her personal story will be a great help to Sara and to you.

– Thanks, Joe. I don't know how to repay you for all your attention.

– Oh, you paid it off in advance when you saved my life.

Mega Clients

We get in the car, and Joe shows me the way. I am totally concentrated on the drive, trying out switches and admiring all the details of this precious gift. However, it seems to me that we are heading towards the coast.

– Would you like a cup of tea? – Joe suggests.

– Yes, of course – I answer a little distracted.

– Look, we can stop at this bar – Joe points to a bar on the street with a nice sun terrace.

We park opposite the bar and after a last look at the modern and sparkling body of the car, we take a seat on the terrace.

– I'm going to go to the gents, Jorge, and I'll have the waiter take our order right away.

– Yes, thank you, Joe.

I see Joe talking to the waiter inside the bar. Meanwhile, I continue to enjoy the sight of my new car, which I can see from our table.

– You like it very much! – After a few minutes, Joe's voice comes up behind me again.

– I love it, Joe. It's a beautiful car, thank you very much.

– You're welcome, Joe. Ah, seems the tea's on its way.

The waiter approaches with the tray and puts the cups and teapots rather gruffly on the table. Some tea spills over the table.

– Excuse me, would you be kind enough to clean up the spilled tea? – Joe asks him very politely.

– There you have napkins, you can do that yourself - he responds hostilely before he turns around and walks calmly away.

– What a rude fellow! – I complain to Joe about the waiter's behaviour.

– Never mind, he's probably having a bad day – Joe tries to calm things down.

We drink our tea while Joe tells me about his tough childhood. After a few minutes, I see the waiter coming towards us again. I try to avoid any eye contact with him, because I am still angry about his behaviour towards Joe. But I can't do that because he comes straight towards our table.

– Listen, when you're done, don't forget to bring the cups back to the bar. And maybe you could hurry up a little, because I need the table for other customers – once again the waiter shows us his lack of manners and disrespect.

This time I can't hold myself back any longer and rise abruptly from my chair to confront him for his inappropriate behaviour.

– Listen, show more respect, otherwise I will complain to your boss about your bad behaviour! You are very rude! We leave when we want! And you can take care of returning the cups yourself, after all that is part of your job!

At that moment, something very strange happens. The waiter looks at Joe, who looks back, before they both hint at a smile that confuses me. After a few moments, the smiles turn into gales of laughter. Ha-ha-ha!

– What's going on, Joe? – I still ask angrily and now also indignantly, because I cannot understand the laughter.

– Thank you, Juanito – Joe turns to the waiter who returns to the restaurant after he has asked me to apologise very politely.

– What's this "thank you", Joe? Enlighten me as to what is going on here, because I don't like to be made fun of openly.

– Relax, Juanito is a good waiter. I asked him to serve us so poorly.

– But why, Joe? Do you enjoy making a fool of me? Please don't do that again, Joe.

– I didn't want to make a fool of you, Jorge. I wanted to explain the Seventh Fatal Trap. So that you'd understand it from the bottom up, I devised this game without any malicious intent. You know, my teaching methods are a little unorthodox, but it's the only way you'll never forget that lesson.

– Come on, Joe. Your methods are a little odd, though. I almost made mincemeat out of that waiter. I couldn't stand his disrespect one second longer.

– Yes, I watched you jump up like a wounded tiger – still Joe has a slight grin on his lips that displeases me. – I'm sorry if the situation annoyed you. You'll soon understand.

– So, this is the seventh trap? – I'm beginning to calm down again.

– Yes, you're right. And like the others, it's deadly. The seventh trap is "treat your mega clients like employees".

– Did you say mega clients? – Yes, mega clients.

– You and your words. That's just like you.

– You'll never forget them.

– Yeah, that's for sure. What explanation do you have for me this time?

– Let me see how I can put it. Why were you so angry with Juanito before?

– Well, I think it's important to treat clients with the utmost respect. You can't push a client unless there's a good reason for it. And even less can you ask him to do your job. The client pays to get solutions.

– I completely agree with you. And who do you think a sales representative of your network marketing business resembles more? A client or an employee?

– A client or an employee? I don't really know. A client...? – I answer without much conviction.

– Correct. It's easier to fall into that trap than you think. Some people forget that their sales people are their customers and treat them like employees. Your neighbour, who's always pushing, fell into the same trap. He treated you like an employee, which you are not. If you fall into this trap in the future, no one will point it out to you, but the people on your team will disappear one by one forever. You can then blame the product, the competition or the system. In fact, you don't give them the treatment that customers deserve, so be patient and respect them. As you put it right, you always have to offer customers solutions. If you demand solutions from them, as you would with employees, they will leave you.

One of the great advantages of this business is the fact that there are no employees, but apparently not everyone benefits from this advantage due to lack of understanding. Without employees, you'll never be a conventional boss. So, forget about giving orders or applying pressure, because that doesn't end well for anyone. Your example of integrity and consistency will earn you success, while at the same time earning respect and being heard when you give good advice to people. Your personal story will be invaluable in this regard. Always remember that you are all independent entrepreneurs working on a common cause. As in any team, each of you will have a specific function depending on your experience and knowledge.

– I understand, Joe, you're absolutely right. But why did you use the term "mega clients" instead of "clients"?

– Well, because your sales people are not ordinary clients, they are very special customers. I like the term mega clients. If you had a bar like this one, you'd probably treat every client who came in at some point with respect, right?

– Absolutely. When I was young, I worked as a waiter, and without exception, I served my clients in an extremely courteous manner.

– But if it were a regular client who came every day?

– Well, then all the more so than a casual client. Unfortunately, it is not so easy to win regular clients.

– That's certainly true. How would you treat a client who is not only loyal, but who also constantly recommends your business to others and provides for new clients?

– Of course, I would invite such a good client to dinner every now and then.

– In my technical jargon, I would therefore call him a "super client".

– But you said "mega client" and not "super client".

– Ha-ha-ha! You didn't let me finish my explanation. Be patient, Jorge.

– Sorry, Joe. I'm all ears.

– Let's move on, then. If this super client brings not only new clients into the business, but also new super clients among them, who in turn are constantly acquiring new clients and so on?

– Jesus, Joe. I'd treat him like a real friend.

– With respect? – A lot of it. – And patience? – Plenty.

– Good, now you know what a mega client is. That's exactly what your sales people will become over time, real mega clients. Do you realise how wrong it is to treat them like employees?

– And why can't we recognise something so obvious?

– Because you forget that your business depends on you and your commitment, not on your sales people. One is to motivate your partners and get them to achieve certain goals, and the other is to get three or four friends or acquaintances into the business to keep it going and to keep it going. This is a big mistake, because sooner or later you will put them under pressure and blame them if the results are not good. Not only will this attitude be demotivating, but you will lose some of them, as you have already done. Friends are friends and not necessarily your best business partners. The only thing you can do effectively is to set a good example. If they lack focus, keep trying to make contacts and recommend the business to more people. In other words, make sure you have a successful Step One. This is the most effective antidote for lack of focus. Of course, you can tell them your story and help them find their personal motivaction, but pressure will only make them leave without saying goodbye. All this seems logical, but in practice it doesn't prove so obvious. Simple examples of this can even be found in nature.

– Even for that?

– Nature is full of living reason. Look at this plant – he asks me and points to a bush in front of us. – It looks very pretty, but what do you think would happen if I fertilised it too much to make it grow faster?

– You would kill it.

– Right! It is not the same to fertilise a plant for good growth as to disregard its developmental rhythm. Excessive fertilising equals excessive pressure on your partners due to your lack of potential customers. Does this remind you of anybody?

– My neighbour! He drives me to organise meetings. We had a great relationship, but now the first thing he asks in every conversation is if I have anyone on the hook to introduce the business to them. He is starting to get on my nerves.

– Even your friend couldn't avoid this trap and as you describe it to me, you have already developed an instinctive defensive and stressful reaction, because of which you almost gave up the business. Memorise this feeling well, so that you will not forget it in the future. By the way, what will you do about the business and your friend?

– Well, look for leaders with real results among my sponsors to support me in my Step One. I realise now that this business is about me and not my neighbour or anyone else.

– That's what I call a response to my taste! Even he himself will be happy that things are going well for you in time. In any case, you are so much more useful to him than if you left the business, which is what it almost came to. Don't you think?

– I couldn't agree with you more.

– I appreciate your attention to this, thank you.

– I thank you, Joe, for sharing your experience with me. I'm just the listener.

– And you don't value listening? So many hear and few listen. The important thing is to remember every detail once you're on the battlefield.

– On the battlefield? Joe, I'm a pacifist.

– Ha-ha-ha! So am I, but they're not. You'll have to fight to stay alive.

– Who are you talking about, Joe? Who are these "others"?

– The battle is in your head, and by "others" I mean the mental viruses that have already been mentioned enough.

– Ah, OK! The bloody mental viruses! Sorry...

– Forgive me if I repeat myself, but it is as important as it is difficult to understand and always keep in mind that your worst enemies are hidden inside you and are the hardest to track down. At my now considerable age, I have watched petty differences of opinion degenerate into real dramas and battles because these malignant mental viruses could not be controlled. Always wanting to be right exhausts a person and causes countless problems. Do not fool yourself into believing that something is happening because you have "a strong character". This is what the furious virus wants you to believe, whispering nonsense to your brain.

– In fact, when people get into a rage, they seem to change their personality. When Sara is upset, her look, her voice, and even her choice of words no longer seems to be hers.

– And it's different with you?

– Oh, man, not so bad. I guess...

– Ha-ha-ha! Because of that "I think", I'd love to be watching you when one of those raging viruses grabs you by the collar.

– Hey...... I...... I think...

– The thing is, you don't see yourself doing it. Next time you get really angry, grab a mirror and prepare for the shock of your life. A curiosity in life is the fact that we see the facial and body expressions of everyone around us, except our own, except in the mirror. By the way, you should film yourself as soon as you start with business presentations and workshops in step two to optimise your choice of words as well as your body language.

– So how should I proceed when someone confronts me with virus-infested discussions?

– At best, try not to get involved in a conflict that could turn into a war. You always know how to start it, but not how to end it. And I assure you, all seemingly insignificant conflicts can end badly if none of the parties involved is guided by rationality. Avoid conflicts. Two cannot fight if one of them does not want to. Take a stand if you think it necessary. However, if you notice that your counterpart or you are too upset, politely postpone the conversation to a more relaxed time. Later you will be able to find a better solution for the problem in question.

– I'm afraid the matter is a bit more complicated.

– Yes, it is, but here too, practice makes perfect. The principle of "learn to learn" must be applied here. In order to get where you want to go, you have to learn some new things, including how to relate to others and yourself. Shall I tell you another little trick for this?

– Yes please, Joe. Any advice is welcome.

– In all interpersonal relationships, no matter in what area of life, it is a great help to have both the Golden and Silver Rules in mind and to follow them. Do you know them?

– By the Golden Rule, I suppose you mean: "Treat others as you would like to be treated by them"?

– That's right. I think it's great that you know it. It's been valid in all cultures, from ancient Egypt to the present day. And the Silver Rule?

– The Silver Rule? I don't know, Joe.

– The Silver Rule is, "What you do not want to be done ´, do not do to others".

– It's the same thing.

– Only apparently, the two rules complement each other. In some situations, correct action consists of "do something" or "say something", in many others it is appropriate for the common good to "not do something" or "not say something". Don José often reminded me of an Oriental proverb that says "the wise man does not say everything he thinks, but thinks everything he says". Carefulness and empathy will save you many problems and subsequent remorse for saying things you didn't want to say.

– But don't you find it a bit cowardly not to defend the position you think is right? I like to defend my position forcefully when I think I'm right.

– Are you absolutely sure you're right?

– Sometimes I am.

– I would be careful about being right, because it is not only addictive, but also dangerous, because you only look at reality from one perspective, namely yours. Some people are right all their lives, which gives them the virus of arrogance. In the end, they have so little modesty that they no longer understand anything. And all because they understood too quickly. Time and your actions will prove you right, not your words.

– All right, but...

– And you think it's cowardly to avoid an emotional drama? In my opinion, a wise man is distinguished by his understanding of how the human brain works. He does not avoid the situation, but simply waits for a more appropriate and calm moment to deal with the issue at hand. Courage does not mean arguing to be right. Furthermore, it is not about courage or cowardice, but about intelligence, and that is emotional intelligence. You control feelings that are about to break out at that moment to avoid a chain reaction. Do you know what Don José would advise you if he could hear you talk about courage in this way?

– No, but you will tell me.

– He would tell you with a smile: "My son, the cemeteries are full of brave people like you".

For a while, neither of us would speak. Pronounced in this way and coming from Joe's mouth, this sentence makes me understand immediately how all the arguments in my life, which came about because I thought I was right, have caused me endless problems. They could even have had serious consequences. I can see myself in front of me, driving like a madman in traffic after a fight with Sara. I endangered my own life and that of other road users. The images that go through my mind are almost hair-raising.

– It's true, Joe. To tell you the truth, it's a miracle I'm still alive.

– You and almost everybody else in the world have been taking unnecessary risks because we made rash decisions. Situations like these exploit the mental viruses for another of their strategies, to spread suspicion. They pose a great danger and usually cause immense harm to people. They attack your serenity and that of others. Usually they start from the negative and want to create doubt in you about something or someone. They want you to get into conflicts. For this purpose, they plant all kinds of doubts in your head, which may sometimes seem absolutely real. Conjecture triggers countless problems and conflicts between people because of vanities. And what is most incredible is that most misunderstandings could be avoided by simply asking. Don't you think?

– Yes, absolutely right. Asking is very helpful. It belongs back in the realm of common sense.

– Ha-ha-ha! Why do you think they say common sense is so rare? As I can assure you, mental viruses prefer to make guesses rather than ask questions. And speaking of asking, please take notes, because we are now entering the Seventh Magical Lever.

– The Seventh Lever? Let's hear it, I'm really curious.

– All right, I want you to hear it. I called it "Question Like Socrates."

– I can tell you, I will never forget that name either. But once again you will have to explain it to me, because I cannot make sense of it.

– However, you know Socrates, right?

– Of course, but I do not know what you are referring to exactly.

– Wow, how fast time flies – he notices after a look at the clock. – What do you think about continuing to talk about this lever and Socrates at the place I wanted to show you to enjoy this wonderful evening atmosphere?

– I think that's a brilliant idea. I love sunsets.

– Then let's go!

Again, we climb into the car and, on Joe's instructions, drive over there on a side road that leads through orange groves. We approach a pyramid-shaped hill, which we head towards. After the flat roads, impregnated with the scent of orange blossoms, the road now goes uphill. The landscape, dominated by fruit trees, becomes more barren and stony. With increasing height, the rocks take on sculptural forms.

– See what a great artist the wind is? – Joe asks me as he notices my amazement at the different rock formations.

– You can really say that. Many of these rocks could be exhibited in a museum. This is a very special place, I have never heard of it.

We park the car at the end of the road and walk the last bit to the top. Not without stumbling due to the bumpy road we reach the big rock at the top of the hill. In front of my eyes, an extraordinary panorama with the sun directly in front of us stretches out. The beauty of the moment lulls us and we stand next to each other for a while.

– Impressive, don't you think? – Joe finally breaks the silence.

– You promised not too much. This place really has magic to it.

– I come here whenever I can. Thanks to the panoramic view, you can watch sunrises and sunsets here all year round. These are tremendously inspiring moments for me. These unusual rocks around us complete the impression of a unique spot.

– Thank you for sharing this pleasure with me, Joe. This is Socrates we're talking about, isn't it?

– That's right, Jorge, sorry. It's just that I associate a lot of memories with this place. So, let's get down to business. Earlier, we briefly touched on questions. As I told you, it'll help you avoid all the speculation that comes from countless misunderstandings and problems in dealing with others. It is always better to ask questions than to speculate. I have always been particularly fascinated by the power of questions when it comes to conveying an idea to someone. The greatest master in this field was Socrates. He achieved such perfection in the art of questioning that a new term was created for his method, namely maieutic.

– Maieutic? I have never heard of this term either.

– Now, Jorge, earlier we were talking about conjecture and its risks. The bad news is that the people you want to communicate with and work with in business have been believing in such assumptions all their lives. Some of them are their own, others have been instilled in them. These assumptions together are called prejudices. The latter prevent us from seeing things as they are. That is the problem. Even if they come across someone like you explaining some common sense to them, the prejudices prevent them from listening. They will hear you, but they will not listen to you. Prejudices act like earplugs. They prevent people from internalising and objectively evaluating your words.

– Forgive me for interrupting, Joe, but this is exactly the feeling I had when I was talking to my acquaintances about the business.

– Most of all, your friends and acquaintances carry prejudice about you. You will have to be very patient with them.

– Patience is all very well, but how do I get them to listen to me instead of just hearing me?

– I only know two ways to get to people without sabotaging them by their prejudices. One of them has already been elaborated long and hard, namely to tell your personal story, if you have one. The second is to ask questions like Socrates. This great philosopher was in fact an extremely intelligent man and found that his arguments often did not reach his students because of the multitude of their mental prejudices on certain subjects. He reached a point where his arguments were no longer useful to him. Then he tried a different strategy. Instead of presenting his arguments to them, he decided to lead his students to the conclusions he wanted to teach them themselves.

– By themselves? How so?

– Well, by asking. He developed the art of asking the right questions to guide a student's thoughts in the direction he wanted them to go. The difference is this: if you give someone an argument, they'll think you're forcing them. However, if he himself reaches this conclusion through his own thinking, his feeling will be completely different. Don José always stressed that the key to this business is to ask the right questions to the right people. Together with the personal stories discussed, the questions will help you to be the best ally. Many people leave a business presentation and have hardly noticed anything of it because you have tried to convince them only with arguments and figures. They did not listen, they only heard. If you really want to be listened to, tell them your story in a way that they can easily identify with and ask them questions in the style of Socrates.

– OK, but how did Socrates ask?

– What would you answer if I asked you: "Would you like to improve your personal finances?

– Uh – [Clears Throat]

– No, don't tell me. Write down the answer in your mind.

– And if I asked you...: ... do you think you can achieve your greatest potential in your current job?

– Well...

– No, don't tell me.

– And what would your answer be to the question: Do you think that if you continue to do everything as you have done up to now, you will achieve the life you deserve?

– I keep silent like a grave – it escapes me ironically.

– And then there would be the question: Are you willing to commit yourself to yourself and your family to achieve it?

At this point he interrupts and looks me straight in the eyes, which, I notice, become moist again because of his insistent questions.

– You see? You are emotionally upset. Without making any statement or making any argument to make you dig down deep, I have done so. I have made sure that you confront yourself, and your prejudices cannot fend off the information because it does not come from outside, but from inside you. Guide people with questions so that they themselves come to their own conclusions, as Socrates did. Thanks to the questions, they will understand that, in order to live better, they need to change certain aspects of their lives to the positive. Only then will they show the necessary openness to listen to your business proposition in order to fulfil this need. This is an emotional business, and the best way to get in touch with your feelings is with a good personal success story or a good question. Arguments and data are sometimes necessary, but never put their value above questions and stories. The former appeal to logical thinking in people, and it is easy for them to fall victim to their paralysing prejudices. If, on the other hand, you get into the habit of asking the right questions and telling your story, not only will you avoid countless prejudices, but you will also address their emotional side, where new and important decisions are made. Say, I told you I don't want to know your answers to my questions from before, but do you think I know them?

– Of course, you know them, Joe. They're obvious.

– Don't you think that applies to 90% of the people in our society?

– I suppose so.

– And suppose, after these questions, you ask them if they would like to know how you, with the help of a group of successful entrepreneurs, manage to solve these problems by getting them a meeting with these successful people, so that they too can benefit from such a business system? Do you realise that I have not yet presented a single argument or told you anything that could lead to misunderstandings?

– But who should I address it to? I screwed up with almost everyone I know.

– I have advised many people with the same problem as you to approach all those who, according to your knowledge, would answer these questions just like you, due to their work situation. I will give you a few examples. The ex-waiter who served me coffee in the bar next to my house became one of my best partners and also managed to achieve financial freedom before time. Another one of my best and most loyal partners is the lady who used to scrub the stairs in my house. You will experience true wonders in terms of the potential of people in modest and low-paid jobs. An incredible number of people feel dissatisfied both economically and professionally and are waiting for an opportunity for professional development, but don't know where to start. This is where you come in and offer them a path that is easily accessible from a time, an economic and an academic perspective. Others have money, but what they lack is real quality-time. We have bred a society of the disaffected where the wealthy have no time to enjoy their money, and the people with time do not have enough economic resources. Since you have studied economics, the term "competitive advantage" will certainly mean something to you.

– Certainly. It's the advantageous feature that sets me apart from the competition.

– Very good. Network marketing offers the competitive advantage over any kind of employment or traditional business of gaining financial freedom. This does not only mean the possibility to earn decent money, but also to create a residual income and to establish a time-money balance. The majority of the traditional successful entrepreneurs can make a lot of money with which they can buy everything except one thing.

– Aha, which one?

– Free time, and in good quality, which is the most important thing in life for me. And I'm not talking about more time to sleep, but about doing everything I like to do simply for the fun of it:

traveling to foreign countries, going skydiving or helping the guys on the basketball team you met. The variety of possibilities reaches far beyond your imagination. Time, as I said, is the rarest commodity of every human being. Very few people enjoy a balanced relationship between time and money, and you can show them the way to make it happen.

– I agree with you, Joe.

– So much for potential new partners. However, to return to our topic: Even when it comes to motivating the members of your team, questions are invaluable.

– What kind of questions could help me in this situation?

– With the right questions, you can help them to identify their personal motivactions. This way you can remind them in the depressed moments that we all experience at some point. In this way, they will find their way back to themselves and gain the necessary strength to look ahead. Their mental viruses will try to forget their motivactions, but you will be there to remind them.

– Turning simple questions into triggers for action and tracking down the motivaction could be called alchemy, don't you think?

– Exactly, Jorge, congratulations. You grasp everything in no time at all. The only thing missing is the most important thing, which is getting everything on track. Like I told you, maps or systems won't take you anywhere unless you make an effort. And you know, first of all, you have to know why you want to get there. Only you can do this work yourself.

– I'm already looking for my motivaction. By the way, you haven't told me yours.

– All in good time, my friend. I hope you'll be able to see them with your own eyes soon. Speaking of which, I'd spoil the element of surprise.

– All right, I like that. I'm a little curious, though.

– Ha-ha-ha! Don't think about it too much, just concentrate on going inside yourself to come up against your own. That's what this is all about. Like I said, all in good time. Shouldn't we be watching the beautiful sunset now?

Both of us watch the sun disappear little by little behind the gentle hills on the horizon. An all-encompassing silence spreads around and makes the dusk an overwhelming moment.

– Shall we, Jorge? – A few minutes later Joe brings me back from my trance-like state.

– Yes, the women will miss us already. At least me! – I'm joking.

– That's what you think. Ha-ha-ha! – like two little boys shaking with laughter. Sometimes I really feel like I've known Joe for ages.

The Stone and the Moon

On our return, Mary and Sara sit on the veranda and raise their hands in greeting. They are in a cheerful mood, which makes me very happy. We walk straight up to them and kiss them as a greeting, which they respond with warm hugs.

– Joe, we have cooked your favourite dish for dinner – the way Sara turns to Joe amazes me. You can tell she's already feeling very well thanks to Mary. And yours too, Jorge! – Mary announces to me that the two women are looking at each other like accomplices.

– Omelette with potatoes and onion? – Joe and I ask in unison and exchange surprised looks.

– You have the same favourite dish? – we inquire again before all four of us burst out laughing.

– Causalities, my friend! – Joe grabs my shoulder to go into the house after politely letting the women go first.

We eat the two omelettes with potatoes, one prepared by Sara and the other by Mary. Both taste different, but neither is inferior to the other in delicacy. Afterwards we sit down on the comfortable sofas and have a lively conversation. Joe tells Sara the story of my basketball hoop, which she is totally enthusiastic about. Only Mary seems a little strange. While Joe is talking, she looks at him differently than usual. Since the phone call that the two of them received in the afternoon, she seems like a different person. Although she hasn't said a word about it, the usual cheerfulness has disappeared from her face. Lost in thought, I perceive Joe looking up at the wall clock and rising.

– Ladies, a thousand thanks for the feast, but I'm sorry, Jorge and I have a few things to finish before you go home. I don't know when we'll have a chance to meet again, and it's on crucial issues.

– You guys go ahead. Mary and I have enough to talk about - Sara's understanding response amazes me once again. Mary's influence is so positive.

We leave the house and head for the lake.

– Why were you in such a hurry after you looked at your watch? – I note from my observation.

– All in good time. Take this torch so you won't trip.

In the dark of the night, illuminated only by the light of the torches, we reach the lake. We sit down on large stones on the shore, which seem to have been hewn for this purpose. At this moment, the moon rises exactly above the vegetation on the other side of the lake. The day today is marked by stunning landscapes. While the impression of the mystical sunset still lingers, I sit opposite two huge reddish moons. One is floating round and static exactly above the horizon, the other one appears elongated and flickering as a reflection of the cosmic mirror formed by the calm lake water.

– Pretty, isn't it? – Joe wants to know in a silent, high voice.

– Spectacular, Joe.

– We came to this dreamlike place because I want to have a conversation with you about dreams. But before that, I want you to do something for me.

– OK, Joe.

– Take this stone. – he gently tosses me a rounded stone the size of a golf ball, which he pulls out of his pocket.

– Good. Now what? – I ask and play around with the stone.

– Do you think you can throw it to the other side of the lake?

– Across the whole lake? It's got to be more than a hundred yards, Joe!

– It doesn't cost anything to try. Come on, don't throw it and whine about it.

– All right, all right. I'm doing it.

I step back a few yards so I can get a running start and throw with more momentum. I don't think I'll make it that far, but I'll try with all my might. After a deep breath to concentrate I run like a javelin thrower to the shore to make use of every inch. As the stone flies out of my hand, I step with my right foot into the water due to the inertial force.

– Ha, ha, ha ... – Joe writhes with laughter as he watches me jump back to prevent the inevitable. My foot is soaking wet. Still, I quickly check how far the stone went. After a not so bad flight curve, it claps into the lake about twenty-five or thirty yards from the other shore and draws the typical ripples in the water that distort the reflection of the moon.

– Just missed! – I encourage myself.

– What? – replies Joe. – You were at least thirty metres short!

– Can you do better? – I challenge him slightly annoyed by his answer.

– That's not what this is about. You'll ask yourself why I let you throw a stone.

– That's right, I'd love to know.

– You'll understand in a moment. It's part of the Eighth Magical Leverage. I'll tell you the name of this lever later.

– You and your secrets. All right, Joe, I'm listening.

– As you already know, Jorge, objectives are about where to go, the course to follow. Now I'd like to talk about the scope of the objectives. What is your current goal in multi-level marketing?

– Well, for the time being, I would like to have a lucrative additional income. In the long term, of course, I want to earn enough to be able to give up my accountancy job. Is that bad?

– No, that's very good. That's the initial goal of most people who go into business on your terms.

– It would be brilliant to be able to send my boss and the piles of paper on my desk into the wind forever.

– There is nothing wrong with that. However, if your sole aim is to make extra money, you probably won't even achieve that. It is extremely important to have clear medium– and long-term goals from the beginning, over and above the obvious ones. By this I mean big goals that still seem unattainable from today's perspective. Of course, objectives such as additional business or the prospect of driving your boss to the devil will help at first. But without clearly defined, more far-reaching dreams, you will not get where I want you to be.

– And where exactly is that, Joe?

– I want you to become the best version of yourself that you never dreamed of. I want you to have the financial freedom that I've enjoyed for years. I want you to have a positive impact on the lives of thousands of people with your story and your role model, so that they wake up from their lethargy and realise their potential. What do you think about that?

– That sounds wonderful, Joe.

– Let me tell you one of Don José's stories.

– Yes, please do.

– One day, when he was young, he accompanied his grandfather, who was considered a wise man by many, to a village he did not know, to get supplies. There was a feast going on there. They both mingled with the crowd to see what was going on. Don José watched as a large group of men gathered in a joyful mood on the banks of a large river in the village and one by one threw a stone in the direction of the river. The grandfather explained to him that it was a game, and after explaining it briefly, he asked the organiser to give his grandson a try as well. No one objected, and the boy received a stone to throw. Don José concentrated, took a run-up and threw his stone. Suddenly they all fell silent, only to be joined in cheers and applause immediately afterwards. All eyes were on Don José, who did not understand why he was so admired and celebrated.

– How did you manage it? – one of the men asked Don José.

– How did I do what? – he inquired a little worried for fear of having done something wrong.

– Your stone has reached the other side of the river. I've never done that before!

– The game was to get to the other side? – the boy didn't understand anything anymore.

– Sure, he did, kid. What do you think the object of the game was?

Young Don José looked around for his grandfather, who stood a few metres away, smiling. He knew his grandfather's smile all too well, and then a light shone on him. He turned to his interlocutor who was waiting for an answer.

– It is my grandfather's fault, he explained the rules to me wrong.

– Your grandfather? I do not understand? – the man asked curiously.

– He thought the aim of the game was to aim at the moon! – Joe ends the story with a smile, after which we remain silent for a while and I let the words go through my mind again.

– Wow! Great story.

– And from this, dear Jorge, the name of the eighth magic lever is derived: "Aim for the moon".

– You could have told me that before I threw it. If I was aiming for the moon, I might have had better luck. Moreover, it is exactly in the direction of the throw. That's not a coincidence, is it? – Now I know why Joe was in such a hurry after dinner.

– Would you like to try again? – he asks me with a grin while he lets another stone, similar to the first one, which he took out of his pocket, slide back and forth in his hands.

– Absolutely. Give it to me!

– You know where to aim this time, right? – he asks when he throws me the stone and I catch it.

– What do you think?

On the second try I position myself a bit further back to be able to take enough of a run-up. The moon stands directly above me. Its reddish shimmer has faded a bit and it is now a little further up. I take aim at it, concentrate, run and throw the stone with full power. Inevitably I step into the water again with my whole foot, but I don't care anymore. I absolutely have to make it across the whole lake. Immediately I direct my gaze to the horizon to check my throwing success.

– Wow! You were really close this time – announces Joe.

The stone didn't make it all the way to the other shore, but remarkably less was missing than on the first attempt. Hardly ten meters from the shore it fell into the water.

– Yes, that was much closer, but I didn't reach the goal. Can I try again?

– Leave it alone. Be satisfied with the fact that you have come much further than the first time, even if you didn't make it to the other bank. The crucial point is to always be aware of the power of great goals. This will always take you further than if you were aiming for the minimum. You will not automatically reach the goal on the first attempt, but your consistency will do that for you. The important thing is to aim at the moon.

– Joe, thank you for all these experiences. I learn so many things that I probably would not have understood without your so vivid and impressive examples.

– You're welcome, Joe. It's my pleasure, I told you.

– However, it seems difficult to me, because if I set myself such high goals as the moon, I may find them absolutely unattainable. Then they do not motivate me, but have the opposite effect.

– All goals are important and complement each other. The short-term ones, such as a successful Step One or an additional income to be able to live from network marketing, are fundamental. You can enjoy their income almost from the beginning. I remember well the motivaction I took from the simple conclusion of my first partner contract. I also like to think back to my first monthly salary, which reached the 1000-dollar mark. Such small milestones have a wonderful effect and are of great help to us in their time. However, as I demonstrated to you with the stone, you will get further if you set your goals higher. Marathon runners, for example, concentrate on each step so as not to lose motivation, but at the same time they always have the final goal in mind, because that is where they want to go. Highly set goals also seem unattainable to you because you have fallen into the "Eighth Fatal Trap".

— The Eighth Trap? What is it? — I'm prepared for all kinds of things.

— This last trap I called "Seeing with The Eyes Only".

— Seeing with your eyes only? What else would I see with, my feet?

— Ha-ha-ha! See with your feet! You really are a piece of work, Jorge.

— Then stop laughing and enlighten me.

— All right. To harness the power of great purpose, your wildest dreams, you must first learn to distinguish between vision and sight.

— I don't know about you, but I only see with my eyes.

— Of course, seeing is a sense that we exercise through our eyes. Vision, on the other hand, is a lesser-known sense that is not developed with the eyes but with the brain and heart. With the sense of sight, you can recognise material things, but vision opens your eyes to things that have not yet materialised. I say "not yet" because the key to a good vision is the complete conviction that it is only a matter of time before they become reality. In this context, Don José always advised me to "remember the future".

— Remember? I think you mean "imagine the future".

— I put it the way I meant it: "remember the future". It is true that if the image of your goal in your mind and the feeling of conviction in your heart is big and clear enough, you will perceive it as a memory and as something that has already happened, not as a projection into an imaginary future. A vision must take clear shape and accompany you day after day. All significant inventions and achievements of humanity have been preceded by visions in the minds and hearts of their creators.

— But then what about the famous phrase: "You only believe what you see"?

— Well, if one were to use alchemy again, one could say something like: "What one does not believe, one will never really see". It is as simple as that.

— As simple as that? For you, perhaps.

– In order for the vision to be powerful, the belief in your possibilities must of course be huge. For the kind of belief, I'm referring to, there are really only two options. The first is "Yes".

– And the second? – because Joe's taking a break from speaking.

– The other is also "Yes".

– Yes, or yes?

– Yes, or yes? It has to be yes or yes. Real conviction leaves no room for "no". And I would advise you to be a very firm "Yes", because you only have two choices, and you're not gonna like one of them.

– What ways are you talking about?

– The first is to increase the volume of your income in proportion to the size of your dreams.

– That sounds brilliant. And the second?

– The second is to reduce the size of your dreams to your current income.

I am thinking through the two ways that Joe suggests, as he calls them, and the urgent and fervent desire to improve my financial situation as soon as possible is immediately apparent. It is high time for action.

– Do me a favour. Please climb on that rock over there – it points to the biggest rock on the shore, which I will climb immediately. From up there I enjoy a wonderful view of the lake and the firmament with the moon shining over everything.

– Good, I am standing up here. Now what?

– Now answer me one question with the greatest conviction you are capable of.

– Go ahead, Joe.

– Of the two paths, I've just presented you with, do you wish with all your heart that the first would come true? – he asks me, raising his deep voice a little.

– Yes, sure – I answer a little surprised at his unusual tone of voice.

– "Yes, sure?" You call that a convincing answer? Come on! That was half-whispered. Persuasion speaks loud and clear. I repeat my question: Which of the two ways should become reality according to your wish? – This time it is directed even louder at me.

– Yes! – I say it very loud.

– I can't hear you! – Joe is screaming really loud.

– Yes, yes, yes. – I'm yelling even louder than he is.

– Manuel should hear you from his house! Yes, or yes? – Joe's gonna give me a little more volume.

– Yes! – ... I scream with all the strength I can.

– And do you believe in yourself and your abilities completely? – he screams like a madman.

– Yes...! – I strain my vocal cords to the utmost.

– Will you use all your strength to make your dreams come true? – his mighty voice sounds even louder.

– Yes...! – now my voice is already failing me at the end of my blubbering.

– Here. Now you get your third chance – he tells me now in a calm tone of voice and normal volume, while he throws me a third stone. But tell me one thing first.

– What is it?

– Will you make it to the other side? Yes, or yes? – He's yelling like crazy again.

– Yes...! Yes...! Yes...! – I also scream back like mad and get myself into the starting position for the next toss.

I concentrate and thank the Infinity, as Mary taught me, in advance for throwing the stone to the other shore. I remember my basketball hoop, which seemed impossible, but which I hit on the first try. I have to believe in myself. I know I can. There can be no doubt. I only have two choices, yes or yes.

– Yes, or yes...! – I yell and run towards the shore.

This time I land in the water with both legs almost up to my knees after the approach in my endeavour to exploit every millimetre. I don't care if I manage to catapult the stone in my right hand away with my maximum available power. As if hypnotised by the trajectory of the stone I stop in the water and follow it. Eventually the stone falls down, but makes a different sound than in the other attempts. After the impact, I look attentively at the water and look for the ripples on the surface that would be an unmistakable sign of another failed attempt.

– No marks on the water, Joe! I've done it! Yes...! – I scream in complete amazement and raise my arms.

– Congratulations, Jorge. I hope you'll remember this moment for the rest of your life – in drastic contrast to the screams of just now, Joe's tone of voice is noticeably calmer and more manageable.

– I will never forget this moment, nor many others that I have experienced in these days. Thanks again, Joe.

– Thank you, Jorge. Your willingness to listen and learn during our days together was extraordinary. I am aware that there have been difficult moments too. But you showed courage and faced the situation, if necessary with your eyes closed, like when you jumped out of an airplane. You should have seen your face.

– Ha-ha-ha! – The memory of this unforgettable experience amuses us both.

– You could already eliminate enemy number one of the necessary conviction to achieve all possible goals in your life. That enemy is called doubt. Don't give room to insidious doubt. It has more negative power than we think because it's addictive. Doubt affects an entrepreneur like a glass of whiskey affects an alcoholic. After the first one, he still needs one. The first doubt opens the door to many more, which you should close from the outset. You need absolute conviction about yourself and your project, my friend. Besides, as I've already told you: why should others believe in you if you don't? It's all common sense. But let's go back to the house now, because tomorrow Mary and I are going to the USA and I haven't packed yet.

– Yes, it's getting a little chilly out here, too.

– I'm not surprised you're cold. You're soaked through. Ha-ha-ha!

We walk back to the house. Near the veranda, Joe grabs me by the shoulders and looks at me intensely.

– Jorge, tonight we discussed some topics that I had only planned for our next meeting. Today, however, we have received some unpleasant news from our country and we will probably have to extend our stay in the USA. Therefore, I do not know when we will meet again.

– Is everything all right, Joe? I've noticed Mary's not as carefree as usual.

– Yes, don't worry. Family matters. Concentrate on an excellent Step One, that's what you've got on the programme for now. Remember, you want to send your boss off to have one or more children.

– With all the lessons, you've taught me over the past few days, I'll have my hands full. I'm gonna go all the way, Joe. I want you to be proud of me.

– Your goal should be to make yourself proud of you, not me. I have complete faith in you, and I know what I'm talking about. You take the challenge with yourself and no one else. You're writing your story, not mine. Remember who you made the famous deal with?

– Myself. Thank you for reminding me – I respond and throw myself into his arms. We hold each other for a long time until I look him in the eye and make an announcement. – I will apply the alchemy to myself!

– That's right. Ha-ha-ha! – we hug one more time and laugh as we do so.

– I will always remember our days together.

– We will always be together, he tells me in a strangely soft tone. But physically we won't meet again until I call you and we arrange a meeting, OK? – he continues in his usual lively voice.

– All right, I'll wait for your call.

Back at the house, we meet Mary and Sara, who talk boisterously like two young girls.

– Ohhhh! – responds Sara to the sight of me. – What happened to you, Jorge? Your shoes are dripping wet.

– Joe's lessons! – I explain, and make the appropriate face.

– Ha-ha-ha! – all four of us laughing heartily.

A little later I come back to the living room with fresh shoes and packed bag.

– Sara, we have to go. This pair of lovers here will be travelling tomorrow and have to make preparations.

– Sara, before you go, I would like to ask you a favour –Joe turns to Sara and takes her by the shoulder.

– Whatever you wish for, Joe.

– I'm asking you to support Jorge in his network marketing business any way you can. He's willing to work hard so that you both can have a great life. But I know that your unconditional support is very important to him. I owe everything I have to this business, but I don't think I could have done it without Mary's support. Your husband can be just as successful, but your help is essential. Be patient with him. Have faith. Jorge is a great man.

– Don't worry, Joe. I've spoken to Mary about this and the patience she's had to show you.

– Patience? With me? – Joe asks ironically and pulls a surprised face.

– Ha, ha, ha ... – with his humour, Joe manages to take some of the weight off the approaching farewell.

Nevertheless, the final farewell is very emotional. Sara and Mary are coming to tears, Joe and I just manage to hold them back. After countless kisses and hugs Sara and I finally get into the car. Before that we also say goodbye to Tom, who has become aware of the voices outside and politely steps out to say goodbye to us. I start the engine and when I see the three waving in the rear-view mirror, a strange feeling of emptiness overcomes me.

The School and the Letter

A month has passed since our visit to Mary and Joe without me having heard from them. I've been dying to tell Joe how well things have been going for me since we met. In just one month I have managed to introduce five people directly into the business. The bonus payments for this have given me a considerable extra income this month. I think this is a good start to my completely renewed personal history. I have established a good relationship with all of them and will be congratulated by them for the great work I have done when we meet. Even my neighbour has changed his behaviour towards me because of my results. In view of my work, almost everyone follows the advice Joe has given me along the way and gets off to a very good start. We now have a team of twenty members in total. Thanks to good cooperation we are all highly motivated and focused. My uplines are very taken with me and are always offering their help wherever I need it. They even publicly acknowledged my efforts at the last meeting. Although Joe has asked me to wait for his contact, I plan to call him to tell him everything. I don't think he'll be angry about this.

I reach for my cell phone to look for the number when at that exact moment, the display turns on and Mary's cell number appears.

– Wow, another one of Joe's causalities – I say to myself out loud before I accept the call.

– Am I talking to Mary or Joe? I start on a casual basis.

– Hi, Jorge. It's me, Mary – on the other end of the line I hear Mary's voice and immediately notice that something is wrong.

– Hello, Mary? What's wrong?

– I'm at the hospital with Joe. He's not at all well. The doctors have just given me some very bad news about his condition, and we'd appreciate it if you'd come over.

– What do you mean? Take it easy, Mary. Joe is a strong man.

– I know, but the doctors are taking a rather pessimistic view of the situation. I'm not sure he's gonna survive.

– OK, don't worry. We'll get on the next plane, and you'll see that very soon the four of us will be sitting happily together again at one of your delicious meals – I try to play down the situation, even though the news has given me quite a shock. – Please send me the necessary data.

– Can you take the first plane tomorrow morning?

– Of course, Mary.

– All right. Send me your details and our travel agent will arrange for tickets on the eight o'clock flight tomorrow. They'll send all the details to your e-mail address. I'm sorry to put you under such time pressure.

– Please, Mary. We'll do whatever it takes. Don't worry. You'll see, it's all just a bad dream.

– I wish you were right, Jorge.

After we say goodbye, I sit for a while and take a deep breath to digest what I've heard. When I have recovered from my shock, I go to the living room to tell Sara about the situation. She is as affected as I am.

The next day we take a taxi to the airport early in the morning. Once there, we are informed that Mary has arranged first class tickets for us, which will make our trip much more pleasant. Unfortunately, even the more comfortable seats and the nice attentions of the stewardesses cannot take away our inner restlessness.

After a flight time of almost nine hours we reach our destination airport, where a perfectly dressed Tom is waiting for us at the exit and makes himself known by waving. We hug each other warmly and I notice that he is also seems seriously concerned. We get on a similar four-wheel drive as in Spain and drive off. Tom seems to be different. His usual friendly and animated conversation has turned into polite and solemn silence, which Sara and I return. None of us has anything to say. After more than an hour's drive we reach a wooden house, similar to the one in Spain, on whose veranda we immediately recognise Mary's silhouette. As fast as we can, we jump out of the car to greet her.

– How is Joe? I thought we were going to the hospital? – I ask her in surprise.

– Come in. I have something to tell you – she asks us, a little downhearted.

The house is similar in style to the one we know. The walls are decorated with numerous photos of Joe and Mary together with different people. Worried, we wait to hear what Mary had to tell us.

– I'm sorry to have to tell you that Joe passed away tonight.

– What? Mary's message made my legs quiver and I have to sit down.

– I'm so sorry, Mary. – Sara hugs her with sobs and I do the same. While the three of us are in each other's arms, I get caught in an alternation of feelings. I had grown very fond of Joe and was only allowed to enjoy his wonderful and wise company for so short a time. It's not fair that he had to die now. I still had so many things to tell him that he would have been very proud of and now I get no chance to do so. The feeling of sadness turns into anger, because I do not want to understand why such a special person like him has to die.

After the first shock and the following expression of feelings in the form of tears we calm down a little. Mary explains to us what happened to Joe.

– On the last day we were together, we received a phone call with the results of examinations that were actually purely routine.

This time, however, something was found on Joe's heart that was not in order. We contacted a close friend of Joe's, who is one of the world's best cardiologists. He advised us to start treatment with surgery as soon as possible. So, we decided not to waste any time and, as you know, we flew here the very next day.

– But Joe was full of vital energy. Remember the shame you caused me on our morning march - I remind Mary because I don't want to believe what happened.

– Yeah, we all thought so. And it was also the case that the doctor gave a good prognosis after the operation, but in the last few days, we don't know exactly why, complications occurred and what happened happened. It is sad but true, and as he always said, we have to accept it as soon as possible. Maybe it will make it easier for you to know that Joe has never lost his good mood. Even in the end, he was the one who cheered me up. He died with a smile on his lips, holding my hands real tight. Among the cruel forms death can take, his was a blessing in disguise.

– And once again alchemy comes into play! – with my remark I bring a tender smile to her, which I return and kiss her on the forehead.

– Yes, yes. My beloved alchemist held to his beliefs until the very last moment. As you know, Joe had a very special relationship with death. He was not afraid of it at all. On the contrary, he spoke of him as a close friend who helped him to be himself. The best version of himself he could never have dreamed of, as he always put it. Joe was the most upright and honest person I have ever known, and it has been a true privilege to have spent so many years with him. He asked me to be strong, to always remember him happily, and to concentrate on being as happy as possible myself until we met again in infinity. At the very end, he told me in a clear moment to tell you that he loves you both and that I should ask you to do the same. With this we can do him the greatest honour.

– I have not been lucky enough to know him as long as you have, but it was enough to realise that he was a great man. There is no doubt about that. And you're a wonderful woman too, Mary. Please let us know if there is anything we can do for you – with my words I am trying to show strength when in reality I am deeply sad.

– All right, but now go and get some rest. Such long journeys are very tiring. Tomorrow the last escort will take place and I still have a lot to prepare.

– Tomorrow? So soon? – Sara wants to know.

– Yes, Joe wanted it that way, that's why I want it done that way. He'll be cremated in the morning, and afterwards we'll take his ashes to the school.

– To the school? I'm surprised I ask.

– Didn't Joe tell you about the school?

– Actually, we talked about a thousand things, but he never mentioned a school.

– That's just like him. I'm sure he wanted to show them to you personally. The school was his big project, his motivaction, as he called it.

– Ah! You're right, I asked him about it once, and he said that instead of telling me about it, he'd rather show it to me one day. Now I understand.

– In the days when we had just met and were practically always together, Joe asked me for permission to spend a few days alone in the woods. He said he needed to look inside himself to find something.

– His motivaction! – I anticipate.

– Yeah, his motivaction. I didn't want to be separated from him, but he told me it was in the best interest of both of us, so I agreed. On his return, he told me that last night, when he was about to give up and come back, he had had a very real dream. In this dream the school you will meet tomorrow appeared to him. It is completely free, but only accessible to children from orphanages. I suppose Joe told you that he had to spend a few years in orphanages and this experience had a strong impact on him. In his dream, the buildings had taken on a very concrete form and the children learned there in an unconventional way. Hence the name.

– And what is the name of the school? – I ask curiously.

– Oh yes, forgive me, I'm a little exhausted. Its name is "School of Genius".

– School of Genius?

– Yes. He always stressed that he wanted to change the world and that the only way to do so was through a new form of education. He relied on the most modern educational methods to make these boys and girls, abandoned by society and enjoying an education based on freedom, affection and universal values, into top leaders in their professions. Following the same philosophy as in his business, he knew that these children would spread his message in the world even if he no longer existed. He believed that each child was a seed which, when it germinated, would grow until a new forest was created. We could have afforded many more luxuries, but by mutual agreement we decided to invest in the school to help these children. That is why we never regretted not being able to have children of our own, because it was as if we had hundreds. You cannot imagine how grateful and loving these boys and girls can be.

– Wow, what an extraordinary story, Mary! – wherever he is now, Joe still amazes me.

– Now, get some rest. Tom will pick you up tomorrow at twelve noon. I've prepared the master bedroom for you. It's all there, but if you need anything else, you can call me from the living room phone.

– Thanks very much, Mary. Go on, we'll be fine here –Sara calms down when they hug to say goodbye.

– Ah, I almost forgot: At Joe's express request, mourning clothes are forbidden tomorrow. He asked me to make his farewell as cheerful as possible, so we'll stick to that.

– Perfect, Mary. We'll come in our most colourful clothes.

The next morning, after a walk around the pretty surroundings of the house, Sara and I see the four-wheel drive from yesterday, with Tom at the wheel, heading for the house.

– Are you ready? – Apparently, Tom is in better shape today.

– Of course, Tom. We don't want to be late.

We start off and after about twenty minutes we reach a place that looks like it's from another star even from a distance. I recognise a group of buildings which, to our surprise, are spherical in shape. At the entrance the inscription on a pretty sign confirms what Mary told us yesterday: "School of Genius". We enter one of the spherical buildings full of people and see Mary coming towards us as soon as she notices us.

– This place is absolutely incredible! – My mouth gapes in amazement as I look around inside the spherical building.

– Thanks, Jorge. It is the result of many years of work and dedication. There's still time for you to take a tour and see it up close. I'll join you as soon as I can.

– All right, Mary. Take care of the people and don't worry about us. In the meantime, we'll take a good look around.

We walk towards another arched door at the other end of the building. As we open this door, Sara and I take a deep breath. Six spherical buildings surround a central pyramid-shaped structure. The space in between is laid out as a garden with meadows, fountains, plant beds and fruit trees. Several paths wind their way through the green and connect the buildings with each other. Pretty classical music is played in the background. We choose one of the paths and enjoy the flowers at every step, one more beautiful than the other. Many boys and girls of different ages are walking between the buildings in light-hearted entertainment. The younger ones walk past us and greet us exceptionally politely between games and laughter. I had expected a place full of mourning for Joe's death, but the ambience is characterised by a strange and cheerful peace. We get closer to one of the spherical buildings with a wooden sign at the entrance, on which the words "Art and Technology" are carved by hand. We open the door and enter quietly. Once again, we are left speechless in the face of what we see. On the one hand, there are lots of boys and girls of different ages working on different technical equipment. On the other hand, children of different ages are also practicing in all kinds of artistic disciplines, from sculpting with iron or wood to painting on various surfaces, to photography and other art forms.

– Watch out! - someone says before I instinctively stoop down.

Immediately something hums past me very close, followed by a loud crash on the wall.

– Excuse me! Sometimes the configuration of the drone is faulty and it gets out of control – explains a boy of about nine or ten years old.

– Well, after the impact you'll have to buy a new one, I think – I answer him as I see the crashed device lying on the ground next to a few individual parts that apparently came loose during the crash.

– Buy another one? But I built it myself.

– You built it all by yourself?

– Yes, with recycled parts from various broken devices.

– Well done! An apprentice of the alchemist. Congratulations!

– Thank you! – he says and walks to a table with all the parts he has collected on the floor.

We don't want to disturb anyone or be run over by another robot, so we decide to move to the next building. The closer we get, a pretty melody, which seems familiar to me, comes more and more clearly to our ears. A similar sign as on the door informs us that this building is dedicated to music. We enter and take a seat on chairs next to the entrance. An orchestra consisting of children of all ages is rehearsing a nice version of "My Way". They must have been practicing for a long time, because the interpretation is honestly perfect. It's hard to believe that there are children at work here. Sara and I look at each other tenderly as we see the musicians congratulating each other at the end of the piece. The mood could not be more cheerful and friendly.

– I was looking for you. What do you think of the school? Mary's voice comes through the door.

– It's incredible! – replies Sara.

– I understand why Joe wanted me to see it with my own eyes. It would have been impossible to imagine the school by telling stories – when I mention our beloved Joe, my feelings overwhelm me.

– Here we leave it up to the children to decide what they want to learn and how much time they want to spend each day doing it. There is no minimum number of hours, but there is an upper limit.

– There's an upper limit?

– Yes, some have to be dragged out of the classroom, sometimes almost forcibly, because they want to continue with their tests and experiments. There is an incredible change if you don't force them to learn something they don't want to learn, but leave them the freedom to choose what and how much they want to learn.

– I congratulate you for your work here, Mary!

– Thank you. Please come with me now. We're going to plant the tree.

– Plant a tree? – Sara asks.

– Yes, Joe wanted his ashes to be scattered on this earth at the roots of an olive tree so that his energy would continue to work here with the children in the form of the tree. One day I will follow him in the same way with another olive tree right next to it.

– This is a very special idea. Since it was Joe's, it doesn't surprise me at all – the memory of his ingenuity brings a smile to all three of us – but why an olive tree?

– In ancient Greece, it was considered a sacred tree. Joe was fascinated by this part of world history and the knowledge of the Greeks. It's also perfect for this dry climate.

We are now moving towards the central glass building in the shape of a pyramid. As Mary informs us, this is where the students' bedrooms are located, as well as a large library and recreation areas.

All the teachers who see us together with Mary greet us very kindly as if they knew us. It is very noticeable that this is the first funeral I attend where no one is dressed in black. Quite the reverse, everyone has followed Joe's instructions and is dressed in cheerful colours, which certainly takes away some of the solemnity of the moment. After we have received a few unintentional shocks due to the large crowd of people who want to say goodbye to Joe, we finally reach the building. I have never seen anything like it before, it is a perfect, huge glass pyramid. Beside the main entrance there is a little hole dug into the ground next to a few chairs and a microphone. Mary assigns us seats in the front row.

– Please take your seats. The ceremony is about to begin.

– Thank you, Mary.

We are among the privileged few with chairs, while the majority must stand. The invited guests and students who, for respect, keep quiet must add up to over a thousand people. Mary steps out of the building with the urn that I know from Joe's office. Immediately I have to think of our conversation about the "immortals" and, because of a subsequent emotional outburst, I have to ask Sara, who has made preparations, for a handkerchief. It's almost incredible to me how deeply I have taken Joe into my heart in such a few days. But as far as I can see, he was also loved and respected by many others.

After several speeches, including one from Mary, in which no eye is left dry, the moment has come to put the young olive tree together with Joe's ashes. As background music, the children of the orchestra that we watched earlier perform the rehearsed song "My way". When Mary scatters the ashes into the prepared deepening in the earth to this version of a song by Joe's friend Frank Sinatra, the ceremony reaches its peak of emotionality. Everyone has wet eyes and can hardly hold back the tears. After the tree is in the earth, Mary goes to the microphone.

– I thank you all for coming to say goodbye to Joe. I don't want to say many words at this point. You all knew him, drama was not his thing, and he clearly wanted me to make this moment cheerful. Therefore, we would like to invite you all to snacks and a good wine with musical accompaniment by our school orchestra. By spending these hours cheerfully, we can best pay our respects to Joe. So, you are most warmly invited to stay.

Elegantly dressed waiters with trays full of appetisers and different drinks step out of the door of the pyramid. Some of the guests approach the freshly planted olive tree and touch it reverently, as if they were saying goodbye to Joe personally. We spend the rest of the day talking to different people and manage to enjoy this memorable day. At the same time, we always stay close to Mary, in case she needs us. When most of the invited guests have said goodbye, Tom takes us and Mary back to the house so that we can rest. After entering, Mary goes to a desk, takes something out of one of the drawers and comes towards me with it.

– Jorge, I want you to know that Joe thought a lot about you in the last days of his life. More than that, he has used the last moments when he was still conscious to write you this letter.

– For me? A letter? – Even from where he may be now, Joe still amazes me.

– That's right, for you. I'm supposed to ask you to read it alone in a very quiet moment. Here, it's yours.

Mary reaches out her hand and hands me a sealed envelope with the handwritten words, "To my special friend Jorge". Just reading and recognising Joe's handwriting brings tears to my eyes. I have to sit down because the excitement is making my whole-body shake.

– Thank you, Mary – I take her tenderly in my arms, and Sara joins us in our embrace. I will go for a walk to move a little and, if I am able, to read the letter. Is that okay with you?

– Of course, honey! Go ahead. We'll stay here until then – Sara encourages me.

I step outside and find it hard to control my breath because I'm so churned up inside. The letter with my name written on it by Joe makes me feel ambivalent. On the one hand, my curious and impatient side wants to know as soon as possible what he has written to me. On the other hand, there is something in me that is not sure if this is the right moment, because I am anything but calm. Looking at the letter, I walk a little and try to relax. Slowly dusk breaks in and I choose a small slope of fine sand to settle down and look at the stars. Since there is no new moon and no city far and wide, the sky resembles a carpet adorned with stars.

This true spectacle of nature makes me think back to the full moon evening at the lake. Just as Joe loved nature, he certainly admired the firmament countless times exactly from the place where I am. I can literally feel his presence in this place. At the very moment I think of him, a huge shooting star crosses the sky, drawing a long, glowing trail and briefly illuminating everything around me.

– There we have the next causality! You want me to open the letter now, don't you, Joe? I am speaking in a loud voice as if he were here with me – All right, I open it.

I open the envelope as carefully as possible so as to cause as little damage as possible. I'll probably keep it for the rest of my life. Nervously and tremulously I take out several folded sheets of paper from the envelope. I switch on my mobile phone as a light source and start to read straight away...

Dear Jorge!

By the time you read this letter, I will have left my physical body and am on my way to infinity. Sorry that I could not say goodbye to you and Sara personally, but things have moved in a hurry.

First and foremost, I would like to share a secret with you. I have always told you that everything about our brief but intense relationship is a causality. What I have not told you is that Don José also inherited the gift of divination from his grandfather, and he has given me countless details that have come true one by one. Among them, he mentioned that you would save my life, but paradoxically, our meeting would start a kind of countdown to my death. He assured me that after our synchronous encounter I would have no more than three months to live. It seems that he has hit the mark once again. I think you understand now why I insisted so often that we didn't have much time.

But well, since I don't know exactly how much time I have left, I don't want to lose a second and leave you a lot in black and white before I start my last journey.

First of all, I would like to congratulate you, because I am sure you have achieved excellent results in the last month by implementing all the issues we have discussed. Don José predicted that this would be the case, and how could I doubt that? You will object, however, that we did not get to step two, and you are right about that. That is why I should like to comment briefly on this issue.

As I have told you, success in your business will come as soon as you have managed to get many people to take a *successful Step One. Now I want to give you a fast-boiling correspondence course on Step Two: "Explain to as many people as possible what and how a successful Step One looks like". As I said before, it is essential that you have completed it yourself beforehand. First and foremost, you will pass on your personal story of further development during the business presentations and workshops, which is one of your main tasks in this phase. And don't forget to continue using the art of asking questions and listening carefully to the answers until you become a master of this method.*

Does step two seem too easy to you? My friend, don't be fooled by the simplicity of the definition I use. You can tell your story flawlessly thousands of times and help many people get into business, but you still can't reach the real goal, which is freedom. More than that, you may earn money, but if you make yourself indispensable, you run the risk of becoming a slave to the business. That is why Step Two is called "Teaching to teach".

In other words, you should be aware that you are not training students, but teachers, who should be as focused and trained as you are, or even better. And here again the aforementioned indispensable and unsparingly honest search for the motivaction comes into play, both your own and that of each of them. As long as they don't know why they are doing it, they will not approach it with the necessary intensity. The motivaction is the key, because if it is not razor sharply defined, it is difficult to reach the summit, that is, freedom. I repeat at this point that it will be of great help for you and for them to know their motivactions when they are in difficult phases and you have to motivate them.

My experience has taught me that people usually imitate what they see, so be a daily example for them and your conviction must be stronger than you are. Never be influenced by people who do not set a good example, and never miss an opportunity to distinguish yourself through honesty and integrity. Exemplary behaviour should always be your business card. Remember what I told you about the mirror neurons.

Your time is limited, so you must be very objective and devote more time to those members of your team who are focused and willing to get involved. Sharing your knowledge and focus with others takes time and effort, so you need to select the best minds to work with them more personally and thoroughly on their development. They will be your advanced students.

For all others who still lack the necessary focus, you will provide sufficient opportunity in workshops and meetings to make them think. Through the work of the outstanding and focused partners, workshops and meetings will be created worldwide. Remember, your business success and revenue will increase in proportion to the number of people you are able to help.

Never forget the agreement you have made with yourself. If you follow it to the last detail, everything will go smoothly. The agreement will help you to be the best product in your business.

Never stop using the magic levers. They will skyrocket you on your path to success and are free resources of immeasurable value.

Do not deviate from your path, because it is much easier to fall into one of the fatal traps than you think. And you know, I didn't choose the adjective "fatal" at random, because it's about your survival in business.

Never forget to thank, thank and thank. Once you get used to doing it every day, you will understand the power inherent in these three words to change your life.

And above all, pay close attention to the self-sabotage attempts of the mental viruses that will last your whole life. I have seen people who have made it very far and rested in their position. Thus, their vigilance was compromised, and the viruses of arrogance and presumption caused them to lose the invaluable aid of modesty for any kind of interpersonal and even more business relationship. It is modesty that makes efficient teamwork possible. It is fundamentally true that this business depends on you, but it is also true that you cannot get far alone.

Remember, my friend Jorge, success is not a place, but a path that never ends. With true success, not only do you gain freedom, but you also come as close as possible to the best imaginable version of yourself and help others to do the same with their lives. Money and abundance always come as a result of this process.

Remember also that every day brings its own demands, so concentrate on the step you are taking. Do not worry about the future, but do not put off until tomorrow what you can do today. And remember to thank your past, because thanks to it you are who you are.

Along the way, you will have difficult moments where it will help you to learn again, to laugh about yourself, to take everything easier and to enjoy more. If you carry the consciousness within you of having done things as well as possible at all times, everything will clearly be much easier for you. Usually as adults we take everything much too seriously, including ourselves. But when you look at life from the last possible angle, as I am doing right now, you realise that in reality everything was a big game, the big game of life. Fight for your dreams, but don't forget to play and enjoy your chance in life.

I've saved something unexpected for you for last. I tell you another prediction of my beloved Don José. Remember the blank, leather-bound book I gave you? That was no accidental gift. He told me you had the gift of writing, though you never really believed in your abilities. He urged me to have you write down all our conversations after we met, so that you could write a story about them after my passing. He assured me that this book would help countless people all over the world. I hope you understand now why I insisted so pedantically on the notes. As I read this part of the letter, I would love to see your face, even though I can well imagine it. It is your fate, my friend.

I feel a little exhausted, and the writing is exhausting me beyond all measure, so I will come to the end. It was a great pleasure and honour to have met you and to have spent these wonderful days with you. It may seem to you that there were few, but you know that quantity never counts for me, only quality. I wish you the very best for your business and all projects and challenges that come up, including the father role. I am convinced that your future children will love and admire you with all their hearts.

Finally, I ask Sara and you to take care of Mary a little. She is strong, but it will be hard for her. I thank you in advance for your help.

My friend Jorge, I send you a big hug and another one for Sara. And again, a thousand thanks for your short but intense and sincere friendship. We will meet again in infinity.

Your friend forever, Joe.

P. S. : Just one more thing. I've been thinking about your future successful book project, and one last proposal has crossed my mind. What do you think of the title "The Alchemist of Network Marketing"?

END

Addendum 1:

The Eight Magic Levers and the Fulcrum

One: Lift yourself out of your opponents.
Two: Use the power of probability.
Three: Use the power of construction.
Four: Provide your soul with suitable nourishment.
Five: Let the system work in your favour.
Six: Give thanks, give thanks and give thanks.
Seven: Question like Socrates.
Eight: Aim for the moon.

... And the Magic Fulcrum: Find your Motivaction.

Addendum 2:

The Eight Fatal Traps

One: To be guided by dream killers.

Two: Try to put step two before step one.

Three: Gossip.

Four: Self-pity.

Five: Become a cartographer.

Six: Believe in your immortality.

Seven: Treat your mega clients like employees.

Eight: See with your eyes only.

www.ingramcontent.com/pod-product-compliance
Lightning Source LLC
Chambersburg PA
CBHW071357210526
45465CB00001B/138